MAVIS

Mavis.E.Drake

authorHOUSE®

AuthorHouse™ UK Ltd.
500 Avebury Boulevard
Central Milton Keynes, MK9 2BE
www.authorhouse.co.uk
Phone: 08001974150

First published by AuthorHouse 01/26/2011

ISBN: 978-1-4567-7371-7

In loving memory of my Mum
"Mavis Drake" love Russell

Chapter 1

INTRODUCTION

I never met my maternal grandmother, Laura Gertrude Watson, born in January 1866 at Goodrich, near Ross-on-Wye, Herefordshire, as she died in 1930, before I was born. She was the first child of Peter and Mary Watson, who themselves had grown up alongside each other in Goodrich, and had gone to the same village school and church, where they married in August 1865.

Laura's maternal grandfather and grandmother were both employed as general domestic servants throughout their married life at nearby Goodrich Court, a local manor house with a large estate, and by the time Laura was born her grandfather had climbed the hierarchical ladder to become head coachman. From infancy Laura lived with her grandparents, although her natural parents lived and worked on the same manorial estate and raised a further six children. Despite not living under the same roof as her siblings Laura was very fond of them and in later years would name her own children after them.

By the time Laura was five years old her grandfather was a senior member of the household staff at Goodrich Court and would most likely have taken her with him to the manor on many occasions, where she would have been gradually introduced to the many aspects of life both above and below stairs. It would have been a natural progression for Laura to become a housemaid while at the same time attending the village school on a part-time basis. Her grandparents would also no doubt have encouraged her to broaden her horizon, especially with books. This would account for my mother telling me in later years that as a young girl she was constantly aware of her mother (Laura) reading everything she could lay her hands on, and that there was always a constant stream of neighbours and acquaintances asking her mother to write letters for them. Laura would have had access to many books at Goodrich Court, in addition to her schooling.

Laura lived with her grandparents until their death. Her grandmother was the first to die in 1888, aged eighty-one, by which time Laura was fully employed at Goodrich Court as a housemaid aged twenty-two. Grandfather followed, eighteen months later, at the grand old age of eighty-six; he never retired from service at the manor. The 'tied' cottage that he and Laura lived in would no doubt have been passed on to another servant and family and Laura probably became a 'live-in' housemaid at that time.

* * *

Just four miles away from Goodrich, across the county border between Herefordshire and Gloucestershire, lies the village of Lydbrook, situated on the banks of the river Wye in the Forest-of-Dean, Gloucestershire. Life here in the nineteenth century was very different from the rolling fields surrounding Goodrich. Iron ore found in the Forest was the life-blood of the village, with two forges operating more or less throughout the century, making tin-plate. Forest iron was considered to be the most suitable for the industry at that time, being tough and flexible.

The first processing of the tin plate began with the puddler or furnace-man. He would furnace the mixed iron and then skim off the dross, the impurities contained in the molten iron, before making the iron bars suitable for rolling into tin plate. The work was heavy and strenuous in the intense heat from the furnaces, normally burning continuously, day and night. Large quantities of tin plate were shipped down river to Bristol, for export to the United States.

My great grandfather William Bevan was a puddler at Lydbrook forge when he married Jane Jordan in June 1861. Both his father and grandfather also worked at the forge, whilst Jane's father was a 'free miner'- a term given to any individual who lived in the Forest and set up his own little colliery in order to feed the iron foundries with their much needed fuel for the furnaces.

William and Jane settled down in Lydbrook surrounded by their extended families, most of them employed within the iron trade, and raised their family. My grandfather William Thomas, their third child, grew up with the almost certain knowledge that he would become a foundry worker in this thriving community, and had in fact joined the workforce as a puddler himself when his father died from bronchial asthma in 1889. A young man of twenty, William Thomas now had a mother and three younger sisters to support. The loss of his father was devastating enough but worse was to come.

* * *

By 1880 the two original forges in the village had been merged into one Company, which was obtaining fuel from three large collieries in the surrounding area. However, due to workforce problems at the collieries, supplies to the foundry were severely restricted, causing much trade to be lost when the foundry couldn't operate at full strength. Trade with the United States, already beginning to slow down, suffered this further loss and by 1890 it was the beginning of the end for tin plate in Lydbrook and the Forest of Dean. Many workers, including my grandfather, were laid off during the next decade.

William took employment at the forge in whatever capacity was available in those hard times and eventually was forced to look around for other work to supplement his income. In 1892 he arrived at Goodrich Court, the manor on the outskirts of Goodrich, and was taken on as a gardener. It was here that he met his future bride Laura Watson.

* * *

William walked the four miles from Lydbrook every day to and from Goodrich Court, and Laura who lived in the servant's quarters would arrange to meet him when their duties were finished and they could spend some time together. Whenever they could they would go to nearby Symonds Yat and sail on the river.

Both William and Laura were in their mid-twenties when, in 1893, they decided to elope. They planned to continually travel northwards until suitable employment could be found. William's mother and sisters had by now moved away from Lydbrook and Laura had never been happy living at the manor, and so they fled. Neither of them were ever again to see their families.

They made their way to Derby, where the iron and steel industry was flourishing, and married in January 1894, when William had obtained work as a puddler once more, and Laura was working as a housemaid. Their first child, a daughter, was born in February 1895 and named Edith Gertrude, incorporating the name of one of Laura's sisters and also her own second Christian name. Two years later their son William Charles was born, named after Laura's brother, and finally on 2nd February 1899 my mother Ethel Jane was born, named after Laura's youngest sister Ethel and William's mother Jane.

By the time my mother was born, work in Derby was dwindling and so the family moved north again, forever seeking employment, until they finally arrived at Stockport in Cheshire, about 1903, and there they settled. Work in the steel industry and work associated with the railways was more easily to be found in that area, and the children needed a more stable home life with regular schooling.

* * *

My mother never told me very much about her childhood but as far as I know she had a happy normal home life where money was scarce but love was abundant. The three children adored their parents, especially their mother, and always referred to them, even in adulthood, as Mamma and Dadda, which usually had a Welsh lilt to it. I can only presume that as children they were encouraged to adopt this little bit of

Welsh language to remind their parents of home. Lydbrook certainly came under the jurisdiction of Monmouth in those days, Goodrich was situated just a few miles away, albeit in an English county, and of course they couldn't have had a more Welsh surname than Bevan!

By the end of the first world war they were all young adults, ready to leave home to make their own way in life. Aunt Edith was the first to leave when she married her sweetheart John Gleaves, recently returned from serving in the army. It was a good marriage for her, John came from a well to do family and had a good job. They very quickly had a nice home in a good area, very different from the home Edith had left. To complete their happiness they then had an adored little girl.

By 1920 my mother had met and married my father, who also came from a good home, the fourth of six children born to William and Charlotte Bailey. William had worked as a stonemason until his sudden death in 1914, leaving his widow with the six children, ranging in age from 12 to 21. My father (named William Alfred, after his own father) was aged sixteen at the time.

Chapter 2

THE FIRST FIVE YEARS

It must have been a wonderful day for my mother when I was born in early May 1935 at Stockport in Cheshire, and she discovered that I was a girl. Her first daughter, Joan, who was her second child, had been born nine years earlier, but had not lived to see her first birthday. When I came into the world, I already had a brother aged fifteen and another brother aged five, neither of whom particularly wanted a baby sister, but my mother did! She named me Mavis, and added the name Edith at my baptism, to please her sister Edith, whose daughter, (also named Edith) was to be my godmother. I have always disliked this second name.

Aunt Edith was the eldest of my mother's siblings and had been the first to marry. The young couple were deliriously happy and it was a great tragedy when her husband John died suddenly in 1936, leaving a bereft widow and their daughter who was just ten years old. I was only a baby of course, but as I grew older I remember that we children were forbidden to talk about 'little Edith's' father when her mother was within earshot. Aunt Edith however was often heard to talk about 'my John' with a touch of reverence.

* * *

Until I was two years old we lived in a community of back to back houses situated around a courtyard which held four back to back 'privies' shared by all. My maternal grandfather lived in the same group of houses, none of which had hot water or any sanitation other than the outside privy. He heated water in a kettle on the coal fire housed in the big black range which dominated the living room. I don't remember living in this community as I was just a toddler, but after we left to live in a house approximately a mile away provided by the local council, I remember visiting my grandfather who remained in his rented house until he died in 1941. An elevated railway line ran right across the yard with the train engines hissing steam as they rumbled across the rooftops. On a visit one day, as I played in the courtyard I waved to the engine-driver, who in response threw a shiny new penny down to me which landed at my feet.

This is not my earliest memory however; I recollect being pushed along in my trolley, (the equivalent of today's push-chair) to view a 'new' house, which we were later to move into. My mother had stopped to talk to someone on the way and I clearly remember her telling her acquaintance that she was going to view the house which the council had allocated to my parents because of the baby they were expecting in September. I must have been two years old at that time and I suppose I remember the occasion because I had caught my mother's air of excitement. I remember she had the key in her hand.

My memories of this house (36 Ring Avenue) are few but I do remember the fuss my mother made about the condition it had been left in. I think it had been fumigated after the previous occupants had departed and when we arrived the windows still showed the tell-tale criss-cross strips, placed there by the council to denote that toxic gases had been used to disinfect the house. My parents got rid of the offending strips as soon as possible and set about cleaning the place from top to bottom.

Compared to our previous home this new one must have seemed luxurious, as we now had four bedrooms, living room, kitchen and pantry, in addition to a bathroom and toilet. Everything was of modern design, typical of a council estate of the period, with a small front garden and one at the back a little bit bigger. Outside, a pavement and road separated us from the neighbouring houses directly opposite, whilst a covered entry to the back garden separated us from the house next door. I feel sure that we quickly settled in; all we had to do was pay the rent, and as my father was employed as a textile operative at the time, I don't think we had a problem.

My brother Jack was by now seven years old and able to go to the local church school, and my eldest brother Willie who was now seventeen was working as a clerk for North West Transport. With the acquisition of a house with four bedrooms he could now finally sleep at home with his family. Much of his earlier life had been spent with our paternal grandmother who lived about half a mile away and my mother didn't like it one little bit!

Not long after we arrived at Ring Avenue my brother Clifford was born and I remember the occasion well. He was born at home and my mother had a bed downstairs in the living room. A midwife was present and even though it was nighttime I was still up and about; presumably my brother Jack was asleep in his bed upstairs. The midwife eventually told my father to take me outside, which he duly did, and as it was raining very hard we stood in the covered entry and looked at the rain and the dark night sky, I holding his hand and chatting to him. Suddenly he interrupted me, "Hush" he said. "Did you hear a baby cry then?" I had not, but shortly afterwards the door opened and the midwife said; "You can come in now Mr. Bailey". I remember approaching the bed with my father and seeing a small baby with skinny arms and legs. The date was 12th September 1937.

* * *

Two years went by and I have few recollections of that period. One day I remember the road was flooded due to the drains being blocked and I was happily paddling about, splashing in the water, wearing my Wellington boots. My mother came to the front door and urged me to stop or else I would catch fever from the dirty water coming up from the drains.

I did get fever, scarlet fever, but whether or not it was because of the overflowing drains I can't say. I remember lying on the sofa situated just under the window in the living room, looking across at my mother who was sitting by the fire rocking my baby brother in his pram. I tried to call out to her but the next thing I knew I was being wrapped in a blanket by a strange man, my mother was crying, and I was taken away. It turned out that I went in the ambulance to the isolation hospital, scarlet fever being infectious. Two things I remember about my stay in hospital, both happening at the same time. My mother came to see me and I was overjoyed, and I remember that when she arrived I was sitting up, tucking in to a dish of jelly and custard. I didn't know what it was until my mother told me; I had never had jelly before then.

One other memory began with a thud on the living room floor. Both my brother Jack and I were present in the room and our eyes were agog to see a packet of biscuits lying at our feet. My mother came running in from the kitchen to see if all was well and we pointed to the open door, through which the biscuits had come. The door led directly outside and riding away up the road on a bicycle was a grocer's delivery boy, whistling a tune and pedalling as fast as he could. Nearly all grocery shops employed a boy to deliver their goods on a specially designed bicycle built with housing in front of the handlebars to accommodate a huge removable wicker basket. The basket could then be filled with groceries previously ordered by the customer. Usually the bicycle had a metal plate situated just underneath the cross-bar, advertising the name of the grocer. We had no idea why he had chosen to get rid of his wares in this manner but I recognized biscuits when I saw them and was eager to try this free gift! My mother however would have none of it and swiftly removed them out of reach. In the end they turned out to be dog biscuits which is probably why they made such a loud thud when the boy hurled them into our house - they were as hard as bricks!

* * *

On the 3rd of September 1939 Britain declared war with Germany and as Neville Chamberlain made his announcement, broadcast on the radio, I was watching my mother prepare the Sunday dinner which we always had in the middle of the day. She was a good cook and we always enjoyed Sunday roast as a family as it was the one day my father wasn't at work. My mother had a peculiar way of making her gravy a rich dark brown colour; she would place approximately a half-tablespoon of sugar on to a tablespoon always reserved for this purpose, and hold it over the red hot coals of the living room fire, precariously balanced on the grate fret which was there to stop the hot coals falling from the fire. I used to watch the sugar bubbling in the spoon until it became just the right shade of brown, when she would whip the spoon away and run into the kitchen to stir it into the gravy, already made from the roast juices in the roasting tin; it was always delicious. On this particular Sunday however, Chamberlain's words were much more important than the gravy and she left the sugar to burn in the spoon on the fire! A distraught cry came from her lips and she clasped first my brother Jack to her and then me, and I was very much aware that she was scared. I remember my brother asking if Dad would have to become a soldier and her reply: "No, but our Willie will!" She then burst into tears. My father was not in the house at the time but he arrived shortly afterwards and they embraced, trying to comfort each other while at the same time holding we children. They had both been too young to serve in the previous world war, but old enough to remember the horrors of it. In due course my brother Willie would be 'called up' into the Royal Air Force.

My last memory of 36 Ring Avenue is of leaving it! My mother had long wanted to get away from her immediate neighbours and had applied to the council to move into a certain house, which had become vacant in an adjacent road. The house in question had only three bedrooms but my mother desperately wanted to move and she had realized that if she offered to move from a four bedroomed house into a smaller one, thereby allowing a larger family to occupy our current one, she would be in with a chance. Someone in our family would have to 'double up' but that did not put her off. She and I used to walk past this coveted house every day on our way to the shops and she would look longingly at it! It was at the end of a row of similar houses and had a very large garden at the side, as well as the usual front and back gardens.

She must have persevered with her requests to occupy it because I vividly remember our furniture being loaded onto a hand-cart and pushed along the road to the new house. On our last day at Ring Avenue we loaded the gas cooker on to the top of my younger brother's pram, now rarely used for its original purpose, and although it was buckling beneath such weight my father then wheeled it around the corner to our new home. Mother was alongside the pram trying to make sure the cooker didn't fall off, even though it was tied on with rope. In her arms she clasped a few more bits and pieces, the main one being quite a large framed photograph of her own mother, the grandmother I never knew. She treasured this photograph and I remember it always had pride of place in our home, along with an even larger one of our Willie, taken when he first started school. He was dressed in his fine school tie and stiff-necked collared shirt; I think my paternal grandmother had supplied the photo and the school uniform, as he was always the 'apple of her eye'. Meanwhile I danced along by the side of my parents, excited at the prospect of moving into the house my mother was so keen to live in. We were off to new beginnings and my younger brother Clifford and I were to have our happiest childhood days at our new address, 12 Ring Drive, despite the war years. We were also to encounter much hardship and deep sorrow.

Chapter 3

WARTIME AT RING DRIVE

Not long after we moved into our new home at Ring Drive, every household in our immediate neighbourhood was issued with an Anderson shelter to help protect the family from the anticipated air-raids when German aeroplanes would drop bombs upon us, specifically aimed at nearby Ringway aerodrome and local railway lines, but some would inevitably miss their target and fall on surrounding schools and hospitals etc.

The shelters were made of corrugated iron and were delivered to the householder in a self-assembly form with huge nuts and bolts to fix the thing together. Prior notification was given to us and we were told to dig a large hole (approximately an area of 12ft x 10ft and 4ft down) as preparation for the site of the shelter. I well remember my father digging his hole, at the far end of the back garden away from any falling brickwork that might occur should there be a direct hit on our home.

We children were very excited as the hole grew in size and depth. What joy to jump into the deep earth when my father had gone indoors for a while! Once the hole was finished to his satisfaction and the earth piled up surrounding it, he went off to dig similar holes for neighbours who were unable to dig their own, either due to old age or because the man of the house had been called upon to serve his country and was now in the armed forces. My father aged 42 was considered too old for conscription but expected to do his bit for the war effort in any way possible.

When the shelters arrived the available neighbourhood menfolk helped each other to assemble them. The finished shelter was shaped rather like an igloo but with a flat front and back. It was sited down into the earth to keep it rigid and also to make it safer for the people who would shelter inside it. Sandbags were then placed around the base and then the mounds of earth my brother and I had so tirelessly jumped upon were placed on top of the whole, in an effort to make it blast-proof and also to camouflage it.

Eventually my father made a strong wooden door with leather hinges to replace the rather flimsy corrugated iron door issued with the shelter, and surrounded the whole entrance with more sandbags piled up on top of one another. He then made a long path of crazy paving which led directly from our back door to the shelter itself as we would be expected to run to the shelter during the night when the air raid sirens sounded and we did not want to lose our way in the darkness, as no lights were allowed, not even a torch! However it was as yet the beginning of the war and we were only preparing ourselves for things to come.

* * *

We all loved our new home with its big garden, which my father soon began to cultivate. He worked hard at digging up the jungle of weeds we had inherited, eventually turning the large area at the side of the house into a vegetable garden where we children were not allowed without supervision. We had potatoes, sprouts, carrots, onions, beetroot and cabbage, finishing up at the top end of this particular garden with lettuce, radishes, fresh mint and rhubarb. Other neighbours with greenhouses grew tomatoes and cucumbers, which they swapped with my father for his vegetables.

The small front garden was given over to flowers and as my younger brother Clifford and I usually helped father in this garden we were each given a bit of garden to call our own. Mine was directly under the window of the living room and held iris, daffodils, marigolds and bluebells. Neither of us wanted the piece next to the gate as this held sneezewort, a rather beautiful copper-coloured daisy-like flower, which attracted the wasps and bees in large numbers!

This smaller house did not follow the same pattern as our previous one where the door to the living room opened directly on to the street. Here we had a nice front door, leading to a small vestibule from which the stairs to the bedrooms began. There were just three bedrooms, a large one at the front, which could hold a double and a single bed and also had its own fireplace, and another large one at the back. The third bedroom was just big enough for a single bed and a small chest of drawers. This was where our brother Willie slept and we were forbidden to go in there. Downstairs there was a living room, kitchen (including pantry) and a bathroom. Next to the bathroom (underneath the stairs) there was a cloakroom-cum-utility room.

Both my parents worked hard at making a good home. As far as I remember the living room was nicely furnished with a sofa, a beautifully polished sideboard, which was my mother's pride and joy, a rocking chair, and table and chairs for dining. Father decorated and mother bought new curtains. Grandma's photograph was hung in the living room and also the one of Willie taken at school; the photograph had been enlarged and framed. We also had a mahogany hallstand, which I think we inherited from aunt Edith who had moved house and didn't want it any more. This was situated to one side of the quite substantial fireplace whilst the alcove on the other side held fitted cupboards over a chest of drawers, standard issue for council houses of that period. The fireplace had a mantle surround, which held a clock, the tea caddy and a couple of ornaments. There was also a fair sized oven heated from the coal fire in the grate next to it.

The kitchen, which had a built-in pantry with a cold slab and three or four shelves, also housed the gas cooker which we had brought with us, a copper boiler under the draining board next to the sink and a mangling machine for squeezing the water out of clothes previously washed in the copper boiler or the sink. There was also a rather dilapidated tin trunk used for storing firewood to start the coal fire and our dirty linen was also usually thrown in to this trunk, ready for washing. The mangling machine was of a modern design for that period and when not in use could be used as a small table (for baking etc.) by folding the wringers down towards the floor and storing them underneath the top. The back door led to a brick-built coal shed, separated from the house by a vestibule, which we children used to play in if the weather was wet.

* * *

The next two years were very happy ones for Clifford and me in spite of the war raging throughout the world. We were aware of our parents' despair at times but they did their utmost to let us lead as normal a life as possible and so we took everything in our stride, accepting without question any hardships that came our way.

Just before I was five years old my cousin Edith got married and I was chosen to be a small bridesmaid. I remember the thrill of being dressed in a long white satin dress complete with matching slippers and head-dress and a small bouquet of flowers. However the main thing I remember about the occasion is going to the hairdresser's with my normally straight hair and coming out with what was known at the time as a 'water wave', my hair completely waved all over, fashionable at the time. I thought that this was wonderful but alas it only lasted for the day of the event. Even so it was a magical day for me, as I'm sure it was for the bride.

I was a fairly bright child and when I started to attend the local church infant school at the age of five, I could already read. My mother had delayed my entrance to the school by a few months believing that as I could already read there was no hurry! Consequently the year's intake had already settled down in class when I arrived and on the first morning I was inadvertently put into a class for six year olds. I was given a reading book along with the other children and I set about reading it. I then began to realize that the other children were reading aloud at the request of the teacher and struggling over the words. Not being aware of school protocol I shouted out that I could read the text. "Well then" said teacher "You had better read it to us!" This I duly did of course, struggling only over the word 'aeroplane', and after making me read two or three pages, off she went to find the headmistress to inform her of the budding genius she had just found! The other children who had laughed when the teacher thought she had 'called my bluff' gasped in astonishment as I continued to read, but it all went over my head, as I didn't realize that it was unusual.

Eventually the teacher arrived back in the classroom accompanied by the headmistress, Miss Hogg. She was a dedicated teacher but severe in manner and dress and although she was probably only about forty years old she looked more like ninety to me with her severe clothes, thin pointed facial features and her hair drawn back into a plaited 'bun' at the nape of her neck. She was also carrying a cane which I was to discover went everywhere with her. She didn't exactly stand me out at the front of the class but took me to one side of the desk with a short tug of my hand. The other children who had all been running wild for the few minutes we had been unsupervised were as quiet as mice now, ready for the show!

She knelt down in front of me. "Who has taught you to read?" she enquired.

"Our Jackie" I replied.

"Who is that?" she asked, and when I didn't answer she followed with another question.

"Is it your brother?" I nodded.

"What's his other name?" I started to cry then.

"He hasn't got another name." I sobbed.

"Of course he has" she said irritably. "What is it?"

By now my sobs were uncontrollable but she suddenly had a brainwave.

"What is your mother's name?" she demanded - "Mrs. What?"

I ceased crying immediately.

"Mrs. Bailey" I gladly volunteered.

She got up from her knees and turned to face the teacher.

"The whole family is the same!" she said. Miss Hogg was a splendid teacher in spite of her abruptness, caring passionately about education. She had taught both my older brothers but as the school only taught children up to the age of nine, my brother Jack had left just prior to my commencement.

Shortly after this I was put in a class of five year olds where we had a mug of milk every morning accompanied by a biscuit, which we were allowed to choose from a big tin offered by the class teacher, Miss Wild. In this class we learned to sing our times tables, two two's are four and so on, eventually learning up to twelve times table. I still use them to this day and can easily conjure up a mental picture of us all chanting them. We learned the names of the seasons, the months of the year - nearly all by rhyme, colours, shapes, letters and lots more. I loved it!

When I wasn't at school I played outside with the neighbourhood children. A few of the houses in our road were occupied by adults only, but the majority were family homes with children ranging in age from babies up to early teens. We all played together in a cul-de-sac area of the road, which we children christened 'the pan' because if one were to look at it from the air it did have the appearance of a frying pan. It was quite a safe haven for us with no passing traffic, (although few cars were about in those days) and one where our parents could keep an eye on us, and also we could run home at any time for whatever reason. We played hopscotch, skipping rope, top and whip and many other games. The older children would often play football and cricket when we younger ones had gone home.

A lot of the families in the early 1940's were of course separated from their husbands and fathers due to them serving in the armed forces but one or two like us were lucky with father at home, due to him being in the age group of over-forty. However, the men left at home were expected to work long hours at munitions factories and such like and my father was employed by a large engineering firm making aeroplane parts. Night time working was prevalent and my father did a lot of this.

* * *

My first Christmas at Ring Drive was magical for me as I suddenly realized it was something special. I sensed the excitement of the approaching time and when, just before school ended for the Christmas holidays, Father Christmas came to school, I was literally speechless with wonder. He stood in the school hall and we all had to go up to him to receive a present handed to him by Miss Hogg. Each present was wrapped, with our name written on it. I remember being 'ticked off' by Miss Wild for not saying 'thank-you' but I was so overcome with awe that it never occurred to me that I could speak to him! That Christmas was the best I ever had as a child, because of course for the first time in many months my parents had money to spend due to my father working, not only regularly but with overtime as well. I remember waking on Christmas morning to find a white pillow slip at the side of my bed absolutely full of good things, but the main present was a doll's cradle made from wood. My father had made it himself; it rocked as cradles do and I adored it!

* * *

As well as going to work my father and men like him were expected to serve the community in some way, either in the Home Guard where the men would drill for hours with brooms instead of rifles, or would learn how to man the small artillery guns on the edge of town, or like my father become an A.R.P. warden. These initials stood for air-raid precaution and most wardens took it very seriously by looking after the community and making sure everyone had a place to shelter when we had a local air-raid from the Germans, and most important, making sure that no-one was inadvertently showing a light on the ground which the German bombers above could use as a target.

Sometimes the air raids would occur during the day when I was at school. On these occasions all the children would be shepherded into the brick built shelter, which had been purpose-built in the corner of the school playground, and we would continue our lessons inside the shelter. The three stalwart teachers we had for the whole of my schooling at this infant school, Miss Hogg, Mrs. Ackroyd, and Miss Wild were wonderfully adept at making each daytime air raid seem like an adventure. I don't remember ever being as scared during the daytime raids as I was at night, because in the school shelter we all had a seat and we sang songs or continued with our reading lessons or mental arithmetic, sometimes games, such as 'I spy'! If lunchtime occurred whilst we were in the shelter, one of the teachers would pop back into school for the necessary food to keep the one hundred or so children free from hunger. The teachers themselves must have been very frightened by their responsibilities but at no time showed us any fear. The German bombs which were aiming for nearby Ringway Aereodrome (now Manchester Airport), local railway lines and large engineering buildings, did sometimes miss their target and fall indiscriminately on civilian properties but somehow everyone took it in their stride; however these air-raids were very disruptive if nothing else.

One day when I was walking home from school with a boy who lived nearby we were suddenly startled by a very loud noise. We looked about us and were horrified to see a German aeroplane flying at rooftop level, the swastika emblem clearly visible on the underside of the wings. As it flew directly over us the rush of air blew the cap from the boy's head! We were terrified and could see the pilot wearing a leather helmet and goggles looking down at us. I was screaming and just couldn't understand why he didn't shoot us, but it turned out that his 'plane had engine failure and in fact was being guided by a British aeroplane pilot (out of our vision because of the rooftops) towards the nearby river and on to Ringway aerodrome, where they both eventually landed. Of course everyone came out of their homes to see what was causing the noise, and a very frightened little girl collapsed into her mother's arms!

The night-time raids were altogether more ferocious and we would be awakened from our sleep in the middle of the night by the sound of the air raid warning claxon. Sometimes the bombs fell almost immediately and there was no time to get dressed but if it was at all possible my mother would dress my brother Clifford and me in warm clothing and hurry us down to the shelter at the bottom of the garden, where we would try to get back to sleep on the bunks installed there. These beds always felt damp and there was always an earthy smell inside the shelter because of course it was already sunk at least 4ft into the ground. My father had laid down an old door and planks of wood for us to stand on inside and eventually, as the raids increased in velocity, a primus stove was installed, as during 1942 and 1943 the air-raids could carry on all day and all night sometimes. In these later raids my mother would have already prepared food and drink ready to take with us into the shelter.

My father was either at work during these raids or on A.R.P. duties so my mother was left to look after us on her own. All the other families were in the same position of course and we used to shout to each other when running down our garden paths to the shelters. Our house was at the end of a row and so we could see all the families running out at the same time. My brother Jack however who in 1942 was twelve years old, refused to come out to the shelter during the night as he maintained that only if the house got a direct hit would he be killed or injured and he was prepared to risk it. I think on the few occasions my father was about he was made to go into the shelter!

One night I remember, my mother had got us into the shelter during a particularly heavy bombing raid and as was usual for us we extinguished the lights and then stood at the door of the shelter from inside, looking out at the sky lit up by artillery shells and searchlights, as we listened to the drone of the heavy bombers overhead and the noise of the guns continually blasting away. (On following mornings after the raids we would search the garden for shrapnel.) On this particular night as we were looking out at all this mayhem, we suddenly saw my brother Jack running down the garden path as fast as he could. I particularly remember his blue shirt (which is all that he was wearing) the tails of which were flapping about as he neared the shelter. We of course stepped back to allow him to jump in and then mother closed the door and lit a candle. We watched as he shivered uncontrollably from cold and fear.

In Stockport, the people who lived in houses without gardens who therefore could not be allocated an Anderson shelter used to take refuge in nearby brick built shelters with reinforced tops, similar to the ones at school, and in addition to these were some ingenious underground shelters tunnelled into the rock face of natural cliffs in the area. One set of this type of shelter was in the centre of town and another set was quite near to us, again for the people who had no other form of shelter. My paternal grandmother and my father's sisters who all lived near to each other on a road overlooking the natural rocky ground were supposed to shelter in these. The shelters, manned by A.R.P. wardens and other voluntary service workers offering hot drinks once inside, were truly amazing. They were a labrynth of tunnels leading into chambers, rather like a coal mine. Each area was fitted with wooden slatted seats and chemical toilets. The deeper inside one went the safer one felt but the lack of fresh air was hard to bear with all those bodies!

Getting there was quite a feat as well and on the occasions my mother took us there during very bad raids meant that we had to run through the falling bombs and shrapnel, approximately a third of a mile, and hammer on the well protected wooden door, to be let in by a warden. The wardens always let us in even if there were no seats and sometimes mother would get a ticking off for not using her own shelter, but everyone was so scared that rational decisions were not always easy and rash ones were very often made on the spur of the moment.

Early in 1941 everyone had been issued a gas mask in case the Germans decided to attack us with any form of gas. We all had to carry them around with us at all times and we had a little cardboard box fitted with a piece of rope to go over the shoulder, in which to do so.

Clifford, being under the age of five was issued with a 'Mickey Mouse' type of gas mask, so called because it was a colourful facial mask with big eyes and ears and a long tube at the front, rather like an elephant's trunk. The children were supposed to be less frightened by this type but I found them quite disturbing as they were designed to cover up most of the smaller children's body instead of just the face, as mine and the adults' did. Once these gas masks were on there was a very overwhelming sense of claustrophobia, accompanied by a strong smell of the rubber from which they were mainly constructed, despite the supposed breathing piece attached. There was a slit of celluloid across the eyes to enable us to see but these very often got misted up when trying to talk to each other. The sounds that came out were of course very muffled. Thank God we never had to use them for real, but we all had to practice often, especially at school and woe betide anyone who went to school without one!

In addition to the gas masks we were all told to make and wear at all times an identity disc. Most of these were made from cardboard shaped like a disc, hung around the neck on a piece of string. However my father made for me a special one out of an old wristlet watch he had somehow acquired, with a leather strap fastening. He took the time-piece out of the case and inserted a specially sized disc to fit, which showed through where the clock face should have been, showing my name, address and date of birth. I remember feeling very proud when the inspectors came to school to check on identity discs and mine was singled out for ingenuity.

Everyone was also issued with a ration book. These told us how much meat, butter, sugar, tea, dairy produce, sweets and clothing we were allowed in each month. The adults had a buff coloured book, my age group was blue and Clifford's was green for the under-six group. It was up to the housewife to make the rations last for the period they were meant to and so they became very thrifty indeed as a result. There were queues for everything, especially if a consignment of fruit arrived at the local greengrocers, such as bananas and oranges. One time when one did arrive I was sent to stand in the queue, saving a place for my mother who would come along to claim it well before I got to the shop door. I stood with her to see what was on offer and she came away very pleased, clutching a banana and two oranges. Clifford and I had never seen a banana before but I was willing to try it. However I didn't get the chance as my mother pointed out that this banana belonged to Clifford and had been issued on his green ration book, which she had had to produce in order to get it in the first place! She consoled us by putting the banana to one side and peeling one of the oranges, which she then proceeded to part into segments. These were shared out equally between my two brothers and me and I think mother herself had a taste as well. Fortunately for us my father who was not at home (or maybe in bed during the day) wasn't keen on oranges anyway and so didn't get any.

When it came to open the banana, probably the next day, mother kept asking Clifford if he was ready to eat it yet? He didn't really like the look of it and wasn't keen to try, but I couldn't understand why she wouldn't just open it and find out by giving him a piece. Of course once opened it would deteriorate, but I didn't know that! Eventually the big day came and the skin was peeled back; everyone crowded round whilst mother broke a bit off and popped it into my brother's mouth. I don't know what he expected but we certainly didn't expect the look of horror on his face as he spat it out saying he didn't like it! Nothing would induce him to try again and so it was offered to me, but having seen Clifford's reaction I declined, opting for jam and bread instead. My brother Jack however who would eat anything, quickly swallowed the half my mother gave to him, as he had had bananas before! Maybe I had also had them but I didn't remember. My mother ate the other half, which I am sure was much needed nourishment for her, and made a change from seeing that we got all the best bits!

Most of the time during the first two years of the war we children got on with our lives without being aware of depravity. Queues and such like were normal for us and our parents fed and clothed us to the best of their ability. Apart from everything we required to live a normal life being scarce, most things were also very expensive. My mother gave us good tasty meals and my father when he wasn't working took us out and about for treats - always accompanied by the gas masks of course.

Sometimes on Sundays he would take us to see our grandmother who had re-married after the death of my father's father and while he chatted to her we would play with Spot the dog. Grandma also had a canary in a cage and would sometimes let it fly around the room but usually it quickly went back into its cage and whistled away with the door of the cage wide open.

Occasionally on one of these visits to grandma's we would call at one or more of my father's three sisters who all lived nearby, but none of them had any children of their own and consequently we were not really welcome in their immaculate homes, so we never stayed long. Each sister had either a canary or a budgie in a cage but we never saw them flying around.

Other Sundays my father would take us to a local beauty spot where he would hire a rowing boat and take us out on the lake. We thought this was wonderful and always came home tired and happy after running around all day.

My father's leisure treat was to play bowls at the local crown bowling green in the park, and we often accompanied him, but of course we children were not allowed on the green. At first he would deposit us in the play area of the park and we would have a great time on the swings, roundabouts, see-saw and rocking horse. Other children would be there of course and we would occasionally get into fights and quarrels but we always knew our father was close at hand so we were not put off by this. However eventually we would become bored and drift towards the bowling green and use the toilets situated nearby. We were always fascinated by the water tap in this building, with a heavy cast-iron communal drinking cup attached to the tap by a strong chain. We were forbidden by our parents to use this cup but we did so anyway when their backs were turned!

The bowling green was surrounded by gardens and well-placed wrought-iron seats, which again we were not supposed to play on, but we were so fascinated by the individual designs of some of them that we sat on them anyway and watched the men bowling, knowing that my father was unable to reprimand us. One chair in particular was made to look like a large fern and we always fought over this one!

At home my father was the typical man about the house for that period, 1930's and 1940's; he was the bread-winner, general repair man, gardener, cobbler and the like. He always involved us in the many make-and-mend jobs he undertook, showing us how to gather and chop firewood to light the coal fire, and encouraged us to assist him mending our shoes on a three-legged shoe last he kept for this purpose, each foot of the last a different size. He would 'bargain' for the leather to re-sole all our shoes and our feet were normally well shod. All clothing, including footwear, became rationed during the wartime period and leather was extremely hard to come by.

Money also became scarce even though my father was working flat out at the aviation factory, but despite the shortages endured by every family at that time, we were reasonably well fed and clothed. Occasionally as money ran out mid-week my mother would take Dad's suit to the pawn-shop (sometimes unbeknown to him) to obtain a few shillings to see us through the week. She reasoned that he couldn't possibly need it during the week when he was working nights and sleeping in the day-time! When, after getting paid at the week-end he would give her his unopened pay packet, she would immediately give him back his 'spends', and then dash off to the pawnbroker to redeem the suit in time for him to go to the local pub on Saturday night.

Saturday afternoons my mother and I would go to the local outdoor market to buy 'good' food, but everything was by now rationed and therefore choice was limited. Somehow at weekends however we had tasty meals and I particularly remember that on Saturday evenings we quite often had steak and fried onions, my mother's speciality. Dad and brother Jack loved this treat and Clifford and I enjoyed it too. We still had Sunday dinner, the next day, but most times this was rabbit stew, which was absolutely delicious. Rabbit was not rationed and so most families turned to it for replacing meat and my mother cooked her rabbit stew in the oven adjoining the coal fire in the living room. Occasionally she would open the oven door to see how it was doing and we would be acutely aware of the aroma of the meat slowly cooking in the vegetable stock with chunks of the vegetables grown by my father, peeping out of the gravy! Eggs were also rationed at this time and it was normal for most families to let the head of the household have the main part of a boiled egg, with the children 'sharing' the cut-off top bit. The egg was sometimes the main meal for a man working at least eight hours per day.

My father hardly ever missed going to work even if he was not feeling well, it just 'wasn't done'. I particularly remember one time my mother tearfully waving him off for his night-time shift when he had a bad sore throat, and to make matters worse he didn't have any socks to wear. He put on my mother's lisle stockings cut down to ankle socks and went to work chewing aspirin tablets.

I thought my father was wonderful; he was stern but home-loving and always greeted me with a smile and a 'lift-up', swinging me up in his arms. Occasionally he would sit me on his knee and sing a song entitled 'Daddy's little girl' and

I would respond by singing another song, popular at the time - 'Lay your head on my shoulder Daddy'. Clifford's song was 'Pedro the fisherman' and father would sing this along with him.

We learned our songs from the radio, which was great home entertainment in those days, and our family was lucky to own a good one, the pride of my parents, and the envy of some of our neighbours. There were many morale boosting radio shows specially chosen to help the families whose loved ones were away fighting, and along with Vera Lynn and Ann Shelton singing supportive songs for our troops, we were lovingly entertained by shows such as 'Itma', Worker's Playtime' and 'Happidrome'. Geraldo provided dance music and almost everyone in the country listened to 'Dick Barton - Special Agent'! Dick, along with his assistant heroes Snowy and Jock left us on tenterhooks every evening. The show ran for fifteen minutes each weekday evening and if we children were playing out on the streets, as if by magic someone would signal that it was almost time for the show, and suddenly the streets were deserted. Many times we would dash home just in time to 'miss' how Snowy or Jock or Dick himself had escaped from their last predicament and mother would have to fill us in!

One Saturday afternoon my mother had gone shopping without me and I was at home with my father. Every week a friend of his named Charlie Booth would come to collect insurance money. Most families had life assurance in those days entitled 'penny policies'. When each child was born a life-insurance policy was taken out by the parents, payable at a penny per week, presumably in order to cover funeral expenses should it be needed. Some of these policies went on into adulthood and eventually served their purpose, as in my own father's case, when he died suddenly aged forty-six. Charlie Booth, being a friend of Dad's from way back, always gave Clifford and me a half-penny each after receiving his money for the insurance policies, and on this particular Saturday I was 'lolling about' on the sofa, half listening to the conversation between Charlie and Dad when suddenly the half-penny (which I had been sucking in my mouth) slid down into my throat and lodged there! I jumped up and frantically tried to get Dad to take notice of me by jumping around and pulling at his clothing, as I was unable to speak, but he brushed me aside telling me to behave myself while he carried on talking. Eventually he noticed my persistence and frantic pointing to my throat and realized what had happened. Both men immediately took hold of my legs and turned me upside down, thumping my back at the same time. After what seemed an eternity the offending coin was loosened and fell to the floor. I was crying with fright by then but in addition to this I was mortified that Charlie Booth had turned me upside down and seen my knickers! For some time after that he did not give us any money, much to the chagrin of my brother Clifford, who of course also lost out. Eventually when it was deemed I had been taught a lesson the treats resumed with strict instructions not to put coins in my mouth again.

Chapter 4

1944

At the beginning of 1944 my father began to feel unwell. He found that he was extremely tired most of the time but put this down to working night shift, doing his A.R.P. shifts and generally working hard without getting much sleep. The Germans were bombing Manchester and surrounding district by night and day and by 1944 most nights were spent in the Anderson shelter. When Dad was not working he was usually doing the rounds of the district making sure that all was well and no lights were showing. On these occasions he would pop back to us, installed in the air-raid shelter, to see if we too were alright. However early in 1944 when he developed chest pains as well, my mother began to worry and she was acutely aware that both his father and grandfather had each died at a similar age to Dad at that time, with heart problems. She begged him to take more rest but he continued to go to work and live his life as usual.

One Saturday night towards the end of April my father came back from the pub, having had a pleasant social evening with the regulars, who included my aunt Edith - who was very friendly with the landlady of the pub. Sometimes my mother would accompany him and on these occasions they would take Clifford and me with them. We were then deposited in the living quarters of the said pub whilst our parents had an hour or so (before dark when the bombing would begin again) to mix with their friends and try to forget the horrors of war. The friendly landlady had a cat which always seemed to have kittens (not much neutering in those days) and we spent many happy times playing with them. On this particular Saturday night however my mother had stayed at home with we children and so my father didn't stay late, in fact he arrived home just as we were going to bed. He had had a pleasant evening and we were later told by aunt Edith that he had actually 'done a turn' in the pub, which meant that he had stood up and sung a song. This was the custom in those days as everyone had to make their own entertainment and 'doing a turn' was very popular. The song he sang was Londonderry Air, more popularly known as Danny Boy. This song contains the lines 'If I am dead, as dead I well may be'.

On discovering that we were just about to go upstairs my father stated that he would carry us up and put us to bed. Like all children we adored this lovable act, both of us clamouring to be first up! To save an argument and probably through a euphoric bravado, Dad decided he would carry us both up together, one in each arm. My mother was beside herself with anxiety and was pleading with him to remember the chest pains he had had only the day before. However he dismissed her qualms, saying that it would be a black day indeed when he couldn't carry his own children to bed!

That night there was no air raid, but in the middle of the night I was awakened by a noisy commotion downstairs. After lying there listening for a few seconds I called for my mother but was quickly answered by my brother Jack, shouting to me from the next room that there was something wrong with Dad and I had to stay where I was and not go downstairs. I lay still, my brother Clifford asleep by my side and whispered up a prayer, at the tender age of almost nine, "Please God, don't let him die". Unbeknown to me my father had felt ill and had gone to use the bathroom situated downstairs and had suffered a fatal heart attack on the way, collapsing into a chair in the living room. By the time I awoke my mother was frantically knocking on neighbouring front doors in an attempt to get help and in fact our next-door neighbour was alone with Dad when he died, my mother having gone for a second neighbour. It was immediately after my prayer that I heard the words "I'm sorry Mrs. Bailey, but he's gone". Those words greeted my mother as she returned.

The traumatic events continued for an hour or so, during which time the doctor, ambulance and police were called and my brother Jack despatched to get aunt Edith (my mother's sister) even though it was the middle of the night. There were not many telephones available at that time, certainly not in private homes, and families always came together and helped each other out in difficult times. I stayed with my mother and I clearly remember being shocked when the police came and instead of being sympathetic to her, started to ask questions, even picking up the bottle containing the medicine which she had been trying to give to my father before he died, and smelling at the contents, pointing out that this particular bottle was the sort used for poisonous contents. It was a distinctive dark green fluted bottle issued by the doctor and probably the contents were poisonous if an overdose was taken. However I will never forget their heavy-handedness with my mother, who was obviously very distraught. My brother Clifford slept through the night, he was six years old, I was a few days short of my ninth birthday and Jack was thirteen. My eldest brother Willie was in his early twenties already serving in the R.A.F. at that time and he had to be contacted and given the bad news. He was given 48 hours compassionate leave to help and comfort my mother who herself was only in her mid-forties.

The next day, Sunday 23rd April 1944, St. George's day, was a hive of activity, relations and friends all having to be informed and they in turn coming to visit with messages of condolence. My mother who could only have been desolate and wondering how she would cope with no husband, and no father for her three children, decided to send my brother Jack and me off for a long walk in the countryside whilst she kept Clifford at home with her. I remember Jack and his friend Tom took me for a walk along a canal bank several miles away. It was a glorious April day with blue skies and sunshine and as we walked through the countryside everything seemed peacefully quiet, it being early Sunday morning. As we walked by the canal, we saw a fish floating on the water, which the two boys thought was dead, but suddenly it flipped out of the water and then with a splash swam away - it had been sunbathing. I had never seen anything bigger than a newt or stickleback so was quite excited despite the sorrowful circumstances of our being there.

The rest of the week went by with most of our family in a daze. My mother's sister aunt Edith helped my mother to organise the funeral for Friday of that week and Clifford and I were sent to school as usual throughout the week to keep us occupied and to allow the adults to do the necessary running around. On the day of the funeral Clifford and I did not attend the actual burial but left school early to go to a neighbour's house where Clifford was smartened up and I was dressed in a new navy blue and white dress, with new shoes, which my mother obviously deemed to be in keeping with the occasion. We were then delivered by the same neighbour to the local Co-operative Society restaurant where high tea had been organised by the funeral directors, to give Dad a good send off. These 'obligatory' funeral meals for the mourners of the deceased were nearly always ham or tongue salad teas and had to be funded from the redeemed penny policy insurance money, along with the cost of the funeral itself. I expect my father's mother who was still alive then, also contributed as it was, for that wartime period, quite a grand affair. My grandmother must also have been heartbroken and remembering her own husband's funeral. My father's four sisters and brother and their respective spouses also attended. Everyone dressed in black and precious clothing coupons used to buy the funeral attire.

* * *

Family life for us was never the same again. My mother as a parent was now on her own, having only her sister aunt Edith to turn to for comfort, although the two of them did not always see eye-to-eye! Their father had died exactly three years earlier and their only brother just a few months after that.

On the night of my father's death one of the neighbour's cat had kittens and as soon as they were old enough to leave their mother, my mother claimed one for us to ease our pain. It was a black kitten with dark blue eyes and so we named it Inky after the blue/black ink we used for writing. We loved the kitten and it brought us much joy.

The war was still raging and my mother felt very isolated in her efforts to keep the family united. At first she claimed her widow's pension, but finding it was not enough to pay the rent on our council house and feed and clothe us, she tried to find other ways to get a few shillings together, not always successfully. By this time Jack aged fourteen was working as an apprentice motor mechanic but he was a growing lad and needed a few shillings himself, so the wages he gave back to her didn't go far. At this time Jack was also eating us 'out of house and home' if allowed, and so the rations of butter, bacon and sugar etc. were carefully divided up between us every week, each person only being allowed their fair share. My mother however sold many of the clothing coupons on the 'black market' to my aunt Edith and her friends who were not short of money like us. It was against the law of course but we barely had enough money for food let alone new clothes so my mother reasoned that we could do without the clothing coupons! 'New' clothes for us came from the second-hand clothes shop, which did a very good trade in those days. I used to wear shoes out at a very fast rate, either by growing out of them or getting them badly scuffed and scraped when climbing walls etc. as children do, and the leather in those days according to my mother was 'like paper'. In fact whenever a hole appeared in the sole of the shoe it was immediately covered from the inside by thick cardboard and so lasted a while longer. Eventually we were issued with clogs by the government to enable us to go to school, and mine were bright red with a strap across the front, fastened with a button.

* * *

At the start of the new school year in September of that year I started to attend a school for bigger children. Having turned nine immediately after my father's death I had to leave the primary school where I had been so happy but Clifford remained there, being only seven years old. One day soon after I started, a new trainee teacher came into class asking if anyone didn't have a daddy, adding that she hoped not! Of course I had to put up my hand and was asked if my father had been killed in the fighting of the war. "No," I replied. "He just died". What else could a little girl say? The 'headcount' was to make sure fatherless children received free school dinners, but of course there were many children there whose fathers were away fighting and whose mother couldn't afford school meals, especially if there were four or five children in the family, so it wasn't very popular with my contemporaries. The families of men serving in the armed forces did get an allowance from the government but, like the widow's pension, it was woefully inadequate.

Eventually mother got a job at a local printing factory to make ends meet but employment for everyone except munition workers was very sketchy and she had several jobs during the next twelve months. As she was now the bread-winner I was elevated to become 'housewife' and did a pretty good job of the cleaning and shopping but apart from basic toast I didn't do any cooking. If it was pension day and mother in her haste to get to work had forgotten to sign her widow's pension book I could forge her signature quite easily and because the people at the post-office knew me, I never had a problem. Occasionally she would tell me to get myself a treat, which coincidentally was usually a child's post-office set, complete with imitation stamps etc., which I loved.

Times were still difficult and we never had enough money to last the week out. The electricity was supplied through a meter designed to take shillings only and that was a lot of money to us! The gas meter in addition to shillings also took old pennies so we could usually afford to cook but not always have a light in which to do so. Sometimes mother borrowed a shilling from a neighbour but always paid it back as soon as she got her pension as there was usually a 'next time'. Occasionally however we would even run out of pennies for the gas meter and these times would boil a pan of water on the open fire and cook on it as well, if we had anything to cook!

Christmas that year was particularly bleak and my mother did her best to prepare us for a lean time. The Christmas mornings we had known before brought memories of a pillowcase at the bedside, at least half full, and some sort of celebration, but in 1944 although Britain was by now winning the war, we all had to endure difficult times. Clifford and I each found a sock on this particular Christmas morning containing a small orange and a shiny half-crown piece which was two shillings and sixpence in those days of 'old money' - twelve and a half pence is today's equivalent. In addition we had a book between us, which we both instantly adored. Its title was 'Sally The Sealyham Pup' and it was such a lovely surprise for us, as we had not expected anything. We read and re-read the book many times during the coming months. Where my mother managed to get the half-crowns from eludes me to this day, but she had done her best.

It was the same the following Easter time. Usually all the girls in the neighbourhood sported a new dress on Easter Day but mother had warned me well in advance that she may not be able to manage it this year. However when Easter of 1945 came I was taken to the local outfitters and a new dress and shoes acquired for me, to be paid for by weekly instalments thereafter. My hair was curled up in 'rags' to make ringlets, and therefore when everyone came out into the street wearing their new clothes I was not left out. How she must have scrimped and saved to do it!

Chapter 5

THE END OF THE WAR AND CELEBRATIONS

During 1944 I became best friends with a girl of my age who was the sister of Tom my brother Jack's friend, and we loved doing things together. We were both avid readers and would read and discuss books etc., once even writing a play and inviting other children to come to see us perform it. We also played with our dolls and played at shop, filling empty jam jars with pebbles to be sold as 'sweets'. She had a younger sister and I had my younger brother Clifford and they would occasionally join us in our activities but from time to time we would 'ditch' them if possible so that we could meander afar without encumbrance. My mother, whilst encouraging my friendship with June, still made sure that Clifford and I played together sometimes, especially inside our home of course. On these occasions we would play cards or draughts and make our own entertainment with games on paper, such as noughts and crosses.

One of our favourite treats was to go to a nearby shop run by an elderly spinster, Miss Turner, with our half-penny spends to buy Spanish liquorice to eat. This came in a circle of coiled up strip of black liquorice complete with a colourful sweet in the centre. Miss Turner usually made sure that we each got a different colour of sweet! I don't remember using our sweet coupons for this little treat but when this was not available we had to make do with a stick of liquorice rather like a branch of a small tree, which we chewed for days on end. I didn't like it very much but lots of children did.

June and I were both fairly good scholars at school and well liked by the teachers. We would put out and collect the books etc. for the class teacher and generally help out, being in our last year at the primary school. Neither of us had a problem with our lessons, except that I could never master the art of knitting! We were all encouraged to 'knit for England' and we were taught at school, starting with knitting dish-cloths. I remember that when we had to leave this school I was still on dish-cloths but June had graduated to socks on four needles!

By the time we went together to our next school, for pupils aged from nine to fourteen, in September 1944, we were running neck and neck, both of us in the top group of our class. The three R's came easily to me and as far as getting things right in class I usually came top, with many stars for excellent work displayed on a leader board at the front of the class, with June not far behind me. It was expected therefore that we would both eventually pass our eleven-plus examination with ease and go to the same school together.

However my mother, still struggling to cope after my father's death, did not always send Clifford and I to school on time, or even at all on many occasions, and it was inevitable that sooner or later this would take its toll on my education. She was very lonely and grieving for her husband and for consolation wanted to keep us with her at all times. Making ends meet was still a huge problem with not enough money and no social security help in those days. Even the attendance of the doctor had to be paid for and so my mother's health deteriorated.

To make matters worse, my brother Jack didn't like living in such an environment and with no father to guide him, decided to leave home. He approached aunt Edith and asked if he could stay with her and she readily agreed. For one thing she and my mother had fallen out at this point, so it was a case of point scoring, and in any case she had always had a soft spot for Jack, the 'son' she never had. So he took his ration book and moved in.

* * *

About this time Clifford and I did a dreadful thing. We had been sent to a shop to obtain some special item and we were given a 'club cheque' with which to pay for it and also a small amount of cash to make up any difference that might occur in the price. Club cheques were issued by money lending clubs, up front, and could only be 'spent' in certain shops, the borrower paying back the money owed plus interest, in instalments. This particular shop was like Aladdin's cave to us with many luxury items and we spent a long time browsing round, with the shop manager warily keeping an eye on us. We noticed one or two framed tributes to 'Mother' and we desperately wanted one for own mother but knew that we couldn't afford it, so we made a plan to steal one on our way out of the shop. I kept watch while Clifford slid one under his jacket. We were successful.

Of course we had to lie to our mother about how we had come by this gift and she was so downcast by then that she believed our concocted tale of how the item we had been sent to buy did not cost as much as originally thought and we had used a little of her money to add to our own savings to buy this present for her. We told her that we wanted to cheer her up and that we loved her. The words of the tribute were beautiful and of course she was very touched.

A few days later we were playing out when the little girl who lived next door came looking for us, telling us that we had to go home straight away, she didn't know why. Clifford and I raced each other home, arriving cheerful and out of breath, only to have our spirits dashed when we recognised the shop manager sitting next to our tearful mother. It was apparent to all that we knew that we had been caught out, and my eyes darted to the top of the radio where the framed verse was usually kept. It was still there, I wondered why. My mother, having suffered the humiliation of being told by the shop manager of our misdemeanour, made us confess and apologise and asked us why we had done it, couldn't we see that this wasn't helping her but was only adding to her problems? The shop manager, having sized up the situation and heard about my mother's recent widowhood was very sympathetic to her (but not to us) and between them they agreed to keep quiet about it. My mother would eventually pay for the item (by instalments) and no more would be said about the incident. By the time he left we were all crying, with our arms wrapped around each other. I never stole again.

* * *

We all missed Dad and grieved in our own way. I had a habit of taking our kitten to bed with me and sorrowfully looking deep into its eyes, my tears welling up, finally admitting to myself that although I loved the kitten, born just as my father died, I would prefer to have him back, even though when he was alive he would not let us have a cat, as he had an aversion to them. Mother placed his photograph on the sideboard so that we young children would not forget his image.

Often if she was feeling up to it mother would visit Dad's grave and take us with her. We would get on a tramcar, which was the most common form of transport in those days and ride to the terminus. From there we would walk almost as far again to the cemetery, as the only means of transport in this particular area was the bus and we couldn't afford it. Flowers for the grave were sometimes delivered to my mother by well-meaning friends and at other times were begged from the lady who lived opposite to us whose husband did not grow vegetables as my father had done but preferred to have a splash of colourful flowers in his garden, growing tomatoes and lettuce in his greenhouse at the back of the house. It was always a sad occasion of course but once we had been to the grave we would look forward to the journey home, all of us feeling much better, and my mother would discuss what we would like for tea etc.

When Clifford and I were left to our own devices we would very often beg a halfpenny each from our mother to ride on the tram by ourselves. We would go as far as the terminus where the tram would 'turn around' and go back along a corresponding track the way it had come. We used to love watching the conductor swing the enormous trolley with its wheel on the end onto another overhead cable and we would gasp as the sparks of the electricity cracked above us. The driver then had to go to the other end of the tram where a duplicate set of driving equipment was housed, in order to drive back. As the tram ran on tracks it could not turn round like a bus so consequently had two fronts and no rear. Our favourite tram had an open-air platform at both ends upstairs and we sometimes waited lengthy periods for this particular one, just so we could sit at the front with the wind against our faces!

* * *

The war lumbered on and 1944 became 1945 with good news at last filtering through to us about the war on the Western Front. We could only get newsreel pictures by going to the local cinema where Gaumont British News preceded every picture show. Even we children were interested in what was happening but footage was highly censored and we would only get glimpses of certain aspects of the war, most of the audience holding their breath and hoping to see a relative who was serving overseas on the news footage. If anyone knew of a neighbour's husband or son serving in a particular regiment which was featured on the newsreel they would dash home to tell the said neighbour who would then go along to the next performance to see if their loved one was on screen. Clifford and I would come back from these visits to the cinema having perhaps watched a cowboy film and re-live the whole thing again, charging about on pretend horses in our by now overgrown garden. We shot each other dead several times a day!

The husband of the family living next door to us was in the army, serving in Burma and somehow he managed to get a record made sending a greeting to his family, which they were able to play on their antiquated wind-up gramophone. They played it so often that the end became distorted, but the record contained messages for all his six children, mentioning each one by name, finishing with the youngest daughter who was by then about six or seven years old with the message "Horses kisses Brenda", referring to the 'raspberry blow-type' kisses he used to give her when she was a toddler. He had not seen his family for four years at that point. When the record was deteriorating the 'horses kisses' kept repeating over and over, and the part where he said he loved them all was eliminated.

By April 1945 it was apparent that the war in Europe was almost over and everybody's spirits began to rise. Even my mother began to look forward to the future, and when on 8th May 1945, Victory in Europe (V.E. day) was declared, everybody rejoiced and plans were made to celebrate with a street party.

This involved getting the whole neighbourhood to co-operate together decorating the houses with flags and bunting and setting out tables the length of the street where everyone would sit down together and eat, laugh, and sing. Each person brought something to the party to give to designated organisers to use for the whole, and we all had to take our own cup to drink from, which would be returned to each child newly washed at the end of the party. A selection of mineral waters and cordials were on the table. My mother, not having contributed very much, didn't wish to attend but sent us along with a small amount of 'goodies' and two brand new mugs which she had used precious coppers to buy for us, as I think at that time we only had one other cup, badly chipped, and very often we drank from jam jars.

We enjoyed the party, eating, and playing games afterwards but we were not very streetwise and there were a lot of older children present so we got pushed about a bit. When we were ready to go home we went to collect our mugs as instructed but found to our horror only two old and damaged ones left. We immediately burst into tears, having been so proud of our new cups and knowing how upset our mother would be. The kindly neighbour could see our tears were genuine but advised us that as she had no idea where our cups had gone we had better make do with the ones left. It spoilt the party for us.

* * *

After V.E. day many restrictions on our daily life were lifted. We no longer had to carry our gas masks everywhere and joy of joys we could remove the blackout curtains! Mothers allowed their children to roam further away with no threat of an air raid and although food and clothing continued to be rationed for many months to come, there was a sense of euphoria with everyone looking forward to the future.

June and I took advantage of our freedom that summer by going for long walks in the countryside or even sometimes walking several miles to the beauty spot where my father used to take Clifford and me before he died.

As celebrations got under way we had to remind ourselves that not everyone could yet completely relax, as the war with Japan was still raging in the far east and our next door neighbours had not had any news of their much loved husband and father, still in Burma, for a long time. Victory over Japan was not to come until August of that same year.

Meanwhile the lights of the town went on again and our local town hall was floodlit for all to see. A celebratory night was arranged with the floodlit town hall, a brass band, and crowds of people to sing victory songs and cheer and cheer! Mother took us along to celebrate with everyone else even though her uppermost thought was that my father had not lived to see the occasion, and I stood by her side as she wept a little. We children however waved our flags and gasped in awe, astonishment and admiration as an illuminated tram slowly 'glided' past at a pre-determined time. We had never seen anything so beautiful.

At last August 1945 arrived and victory in the Far East was announced, with even more celebrations throughout the country. The celebratory day this time was named V.J. Day - victory over Japan.

At this stage most people thought that all service men and women would be quickly re-united with their families and we could all get on with our lives once more, but it was to be well into 1946 before our troops would arrive home and then only in small batches.

Just before Christmas 1945 my brother Willie (by now called Bill by his contemporaries) arranged to get married. He had met his bride Evalina, whose home- town was Bromborough on the Wirral peninsular, when they were both serving in the R.A.F. and stationed at Blackpool. He had brought her home to meet his family at the end of the war but apart from that visit we didn't have much contact with her until it was time to arrange the wedding. I was chosen to be a small bridesmaid, along with two of her W.R.A.F. friends and was taken to Manchester, where the shops were beginning to open up again with all sorts of goodies, to buy a suitable bridesmaid dress for me. Mine was the only new dress for the occasion and probably used up most of the extra clothing coupons issued by the government when service personnel were getting married. The bride's dress and the two adult bridesmaid ones were borrowed from a 'pool' of up-market gowns previously worn by film stars, socialites and the like, and contributed to the 'pool' as part of the war effort. Bill and Eve were married in the bride's home- town and we had to travel there by train, via Liverpool.

The wedding was a great success and even my grandmother made the journey as Bill was her favourite grandson and they shared a close relationship. After the service and celebrations we made our way back to Stockport while the happy couple set off on their honeymoon, prior to rejoining their R.A.F. unit until demobilisation some months later.

* * *

By the time 1946 dawned most families could see a light at the end of the tunnel. Food was more plentiful and rationing on as many items as possible relaxed, but not eliminated.

June and I continued our friendship, both of us spending many happy days at our local library. We were both avid readers and usually averaged a book a day in winter.

Sometime in the early part of that year all children in our age group sat the eleven-plus examination. The examination consisted of two parts and if one didn't pass the first part, one didn't even get a chance to sit the second part, which was the passport to grammar school.

The examination was held at the town hall on a Saturday morning and was compulsory. A room was set out with single desks and chairs, each unit kitted out with pen and pencil etc. We were issued with examination papers for each subject in turn and given a time limit to complete each paper, watched over by the examiners. Arithmetic was first and I quickly had all the sums neatly and correctly finished and knew that I didn't even need to check them; they had been quite easy. On seeing my idle hands the examiner broke the silence rule by asking me why I was not working, whereupon I told him that I had finished. I could tell by his face when he picked up my paper that he was surprised. English and general knowledge followed and they too were easy. Of course afterwards we children, especially June and I compared notes and were in agreement. We both thought we would now go to grammar school together once we had taken the second part of the examination.

A few weeks later when I rushed home from school to tell my mother that I had been informed at school that I had passed the examination, I was very disappointed by her non-committal remarks. It turned out that she was deeply troubled because she knew that she would not be able to afford the school uniform, compulsory for the grammar school. In the event it didn't matter because I failed the second examination due to lack of general knowledge, having been absent from school so much since my father died. I was very disappointed.

One day everyone in our street was scurrying around buying flags and bunting because at long last our neighbours next door were expecting their loved one home. My mother did not have any coppers with which to buy a flag and had not managed to borrow one and she felt rather ashamed to be the only house without a homecoming tribute. However I clearly remember the soldier walking the length of the street amid much cheering and clapping, and as he took his wife in his arms in the street I don't suppose he noticed! He had not seen his family for five years, had lost much weight, and was soon whisked indoors for a private reunion.

Chapter 6

1946

Before the war, like many other towns and cities across Britain, Stockport had held a yearly street carnival during the summer months in aid of local charities, which of course had to be suspended after the outbreak of war. It was resumed in the summer of 1946 after a break of five or six years and caused much excitement; the whole town seemed to turn out to celebrate. Clifford and I had no idea what was in store for us but as we made our way with our mother to view the procession, almost from the same spot that we had observed the flood-lit town hall a year earlier, we could hardly grasp the enormity of the event. Everyone seemed to be waving a hand-held paper union flag, street-sellers were everywhere selling carnival whistles, hats and the like and people thronged the pavements waiting in anticipation for the start of the procession. Our mother managed to find a place for us at the edge of the pavement where we had a good vantage point and she could stand directly behind us, encouraging us to look this way and that way.

The floats took my breath away with their glamour! They were actually flat-backed lorries but when my eyes alighted on the queens and their entourages from various local churches, the lorries could have been golden coaches. We were used to the austerity of war, an austerity still prevalent a year or so later, so the sight of red velvet cloaks and white satin dresses, all enriched by floral displays, was like something from another world to me. We cheered until we were hoarse and all the time clowns and people in animal costumes etc. would walk past us rattling their collection tins, or even holding an umbrella upside down so that we could throw coppers into it. We had each been given five separate halfpennies and told to choose our favourite representative for the various charities, my mother doing her best to encourage us to wait and see who came next. All the families walked home together afterwards, the grown-ups reminiscing and we children still excitedly discussing which particular float we had liked best. I will never forget the glamour and excitement of that day.

* * *

Another memorable activity resumed after the war was the organising of day trips by train to the coastal resorts of Blackpool, Southport, Morecambe and New Brighton. These trains began to run again on one day each week of the school holidays and because nearly all families participated in at least one event my mother somehow was able to take us. She had probably 'sold' our clothing coupons to my aunt in order to afford the trip, as I remember discussing this with other people in the queue for the train tickets and was quickly rounded upon by both my mother and my aunt,who was accompanying us that day, and told to "keep quiet!"; of course I didn't know it was illegal.

We could only afford one trip and went to Blackpool, where we had a wonderful time. We were able to try the slot machines and rides on the fun fair, all of which were first time experiences for us. My mother drew the line at buying me a paper hat with "kiss me quick" on it, saying that it was a waste of money.

Not many children had swimming costumes in those days, most did as I was told to do when I went paddling in the sea - tuck my dress inside my knickers! Everyone did the same so it wasn't all that embarrassing. I had only ever seen the sea once before when I was about four or five years old and aunt Edith took me and my brother Jack to Southport for the day. On that occasion I was terrified of the sea and screamed blue murder at the thought of walking in it! It was only about five or six inches deep but seemed to me to stretch to eternity, and I would not go in. We had probably walked a mile or so down the beach first, in order to reach the sea at Southport, and I remember my aunt giving Jack the shoes etc. to carry, whilst she carried me! However I was by now four or five years older and all my friends were splashing about in it, so I joined in!

* * *

Another joyous occasion I remember that year was the fun fair coming to a local park. My mother allowed Clifford and I to go on ahead of her, which involved a tram ride followed by a walk through the park to get to the fairground. We had been given a few coppers and had been ordered to stay together and keep clean; mother would join us later on and provided we stayed in the park she would find us. Most of the local families would be there and so we would not be short of company.

After alighting from the tram, on our walk to the fairground we had to pass a pond where I vaguely remembered my father had made paper boats for Clifford and me to set upon the water. However the pond this time looked dried up and abandoned, being covered in a coating of what I thought was moss, but turned out to be algae! It was difficult to decide at the edge of the pond due to the many weeds choking the bank but I was confident that it was hard turf and demonstrated to my brother how I could walk on it! Of course before I knew it my foot and leg had disappeared in the green slime and one of my new white socks and shoes covered in the stuff. I was lucky not to have gone in much deeper and probably would have done so if Clifford had not been pulling me back by the hand.

* * *

As summer turned to autumn that year my mother did her best to look after us but although she managed to get work from time to time, she struggled to cope. By this time the three of us were on our own, my brother Jack having gone to live with aunt

Edith, and my brother Bill and his wife Eve who, after being demobbed from the air-force lived with us for a short time, had by now found lodgings (two rooms and use of kitchen and bathroom) in a more residential area of Stockport, where they could have some privacy and entertain friends etc. By this time also they were expecting their first child.

As Christmas approached things were looking bleak; money was scarce, and our well-being, making sure that we were not hungry, and keeping us warm, was my mother's prime concern. Coal was still rationed and of poor quality. Coke was easier to obtain but difficult to burn and even that was rationed - it was a kind of cinder made from scrapings of legitimate coal. Occasionally we could buy coal 'eggs' - an egg-shaped pat of compressed coal dust, which many times put out whatever fire we had managed to make!

Food was usually obtained 'on tick' (meaning it would be paid for at a later date) from a kindly local grocer who knew my mother's circumstances, but even so the grocer kept a wary eye on us. Mother always made sure we had our rations and would do her best to make tasty meals with whatever was available but we were nearly always hungry. Whenever I was sent to the shop for a loaf of bread I would almost always bite off each corner of the loaf on my way home, even though I had been told not to do so by mother and promised the first slice when I got home! Once home Clifford and I quickly devoured the loaf if we weren't restrained by mother who of course wanted to save half of it for the following day. She would give us jam and bread when available, (jam was still rationed but could be obtained in lieu of sugar) or condensed milk on bread - a sticky substance, very sweet and milky, which was really meant to be used as a substitute for sugar and milk in hot drinks. If we had bacon 'butties' one day, we had 'dip butties' the next - 'dip' being the residue fat still left in the frying pan after cooking the bacon. Mother always gave us two slices each (because we were hungry) before having one herself.

* * *

Towards the end of 1946 my paternal grandmother died. Since my father's death two years earlier we had not had much contact with his relatives but my brother Bill had kept up his own social visits to his 'grandma' as they were very fond of each other.

I remember that Clifford and I were at home on our own the day my father's brother and one of his sisters came to tell us of their mother's death and inform us of the funeral arrangements; my mother was at work.

Our circumstances by that time were very rocky to say the least but whenever mother could find work I always took on the role of 'little mother' keeping the house tidy etc. Unfortunately on that day as they arrived with the sad news quite early in the morning I had not yet tidied up, as like any child I preferred to play first and make sure all jobs were done before mother came home. She was very upset when she did arrive home, not so much at grandma's demise but because father's relatives had seen how we were living. We did not attend the funeral, I think mother sent flowers and went to work whilst it was available. When I look back now I realise that although our circumstances must have been apparent, no offer of help came from that quarter. Perhaps they thought that if mother was working we had enough money to get by, but working days were few and far between and her widow's pension was far from adequate.

Chapter 7

1947

The weather in the winter of 1946/7 was extremely ferocious. It was bitterly cold and if it wasn't raining it was snowing, and then the snow would freeze over, making any attempt to go out very hazardous. We had to dig out a path from door to gate somehow and this was difficult, as at times the heavy snow formed drifts of up to 4ft deep. If my mother or I did venture out we had to share the only pair of shoes we had. By that time I had outgrown the clogs issued by the council and my feet were the same size as mother's - size four! If one of us went out the other one stayed at home. Some of the children had Wellington boots but I don't think our budget ran to it, as I don't remember having any.

Everything was difficult to come by, especially fuel for our fire, which was our only form of heating. The main thing I remember about the cold weather in 1947 is that we often pushed an old pram up to the railway sidings to join other families scrabbling amongst heaps of coal dust in the open coal yard to pick out any small pieces of coal that had escaped the eye of the men who bagged the decent coal ready for distribution to householders - if they were lucky! Whenever a member of staff at the sidings observed us we were sent away, but if they did not lock the gates to the yard we would all hide around the corner until the coast was clear. The tiny bits of coal we managed to accumulate were called 'nutty slack'. Of course by the time we got home we were cold and hungry and needed a good wash or a bath; if we had no coal for the fire we would have to heat up pans of hot water on the gas cooker, hence my mother's preference for gas against electricity. Sometimes we pushed the pram up to the coal-yard in order to <u>buy</u> a bag of coal, coke, or even nutty slack with money saved for this purpose, but very often it just wasn't available.

My mother could not find work during this period so often we didn't have enough money for heating <u>and</u> lighting. Mother would always opt to put pennies in the gas meter rather than a shilling for electricity as she maintained that as long as we could cook and make a pot of tea, we could do everything else by candlelight.

One night the house was in darkness and we had all been sitting around the last embers of our fire, prior to going to bed. Mother had been 'entertaining' us as usual by talking to us as we sat in our little group. She would point out 'faces' made by the cinders in the embers and tell us stories. As the fire was dying we were going to go to bed to keep warm and to do so we were all going to sleep together in one big double bed. In addition mother had warmed a flat iron and a baking tray in the oven heated by the coal fire, to take to bed to warm our feet - rather like a hot-water bottle. As we only had one candle available I was to carry it upstairs to light the way whilst she carried the warmed irons. All went well until

I deposited the candlestick containing the lit candle onto the window sill and left it unattended. Mother had gone to the bathroom, situated downstairs, and as I left the bedroom, pulling the door shut as I left, it caused a draught, which in turn wafted the candle and set the curtains alight. When I returned to the bedroom I was confronted with the sight of the whole window in flames, and I screamed for mother. At the same time someone was banging on the front door to alert us, as the flames had been seen by neighbours. The fire was quickly put out by helping hands carrying buckets of water and such like, but mother was in a state of shock and weakly collapsed into a chair.

* * *

As that terrible winter progressed mother was desperate for money to feed and clothe us and keep us warm. She looked around the house to assess the value of anything worth selling. The first thing to go was our lovely polished sideboard, mother's pride and joy. It was the nicest thing we had but we could manage without it. It was the first of many of our possessions to be sold to a local second-hand goods dealer who benefited greatly from our dire circumstances. I remember his advertising slogan was 'Eye buy anything' with a picture of a big eye, followed by his name. My mother hated him but felt she had no other option if we were to survive. Of course he didn't pay us anything like the true value of our goods. After each sale we would celebrate with 'real' food and a visit to the second-hand clothes shop, weather permitting. Now at least we could have electric light and listen to the radio.

Eventually mother had either sold or chopped up with an axe for firewood, nearly everything that we owned. We would sit in front of the fire watching as chair legs were burned, followed by old shoes, old linoleum, anything that would keep us warm. We were left with only one bed, which we shared, and just enough furniture to cosily fit out the kitchen as a small living area. We had everything we needed, the gas cooker kept us warm (mother would light the oven and open the door) we used the table-top mangle as a table and she had kept a comfortable chair and a few other bits and pieces. The living room was now devoid of all furniture with no carpet on the floor.

Of course things were rapidly sliding downhill and somehow my brother Bill got wind of this and paid us a visit. He had obviously come to see for himself if the rumours were correct. He was appalled and took mother into the empty living room, whereupon we followed to see what was going on. We were just in time to hear him say "You can't go on like this" before he sent us back into the kitchen. Mother was in tears and when he asked us if we liked living in the kitchen we assured him that we did. What we didn't like was to see our mother sobbing.

About a week later an official from the N.S.P.C.C. paid us a visit. Unfortunately for my mother, when he arrived Clifford and I were having a wonderful time jumping on the coil spring based bed, which enabled us to bounce beautifully - rather like a trampoline. We were in high spirits and had got into a giddy mood, thoroughly enjoying ourselves, not even aware that we were being watched by the adults, from the doorway. When we did see them we stopped jumping but carried on laughing, a bit hysterically. We must have looked like very unruly children, completely out of control, when in reality it was a mad half hour where we were letting off steam. We should probably have been at school however, but by this time mother didn't bother to send us. She just stood there, near to tears and wringing her hands, attempting to explain to the onlooker that we were not badly behaved and certainly not unloved. We did not realise the seriousness of the situation and carried on laughing. Afterwards she cried endlessly; mortified that the neighbours would have witnessed the visit and most of all she just could not believe that her beloved eldest son had obviously informed the authorities of our plight, without giving her a chance - as she saw it, to get back on her feet. Of course this would have been nigh on impossible. None of us knew that she was on the brink of a nervous breakdown.

* * *

The rent on our council house had not been paid for many months and we had been threatened with eviction. Mother must have known that it was about to happen because she contacted the second-hand goods dealer a day or so before the event and sold him the last of our belongings. By now they were very meagre so he didn't bother to send a van for them but instead used a horse-drawn cart, bearing no identification. We had always been instructed not to let on to the neighbours just what difficulties we faced and so I never told the truth. Mother had sent us out to play when the dealer came and I had told my friends that we were moving house. One of them said that she had just seen our furniture being moved and I agreed with her that it was being taken to our next home.

Eventually however we were left with just personal possessions and mother must have known it was the end of the road for us. She packed the best of her possessions in the old tin trunk where we had in the past kept firewood and dirty laundry, and asked a kindly neighbour if she could leave it by her back door until such time as she could collect it again. The neighbour reluctantly agreed and so my mother's treasured possessions were left - framed photographs of my father and her own mother and a couple of good blankets, which I think had been given to us, along with a few other sentimental belongings. They were never to be retrieved.

Shortly afterwards the evictors came, marched in, and started throwing things out of the bedroom window onto the back garden. I was horrified that they were throwing good stuff down and mother wasn't doing anything about it, but between tears she told me that it didn't matter that they were throwing her best shoes out, as we would get some more. She then dressed us in our best clothes - mine being quite presentable as I had recently been given a whole new set, consisting of coat, dress and jacket, from a good Samaritan who must have been told of our plight and had no further use for them.

Once we had gathered our few belongings together we were ordered off the premises and I was sent to put a few last minute items into the tin trunk. The kindly neighbour had by now been taken into my mother's confidence and realised that we had no definite place to go; mother was going to seek help. When I finally closed the trunk she handed me two and a half old pennies, this being the price of a postage stamp. She explained that she had not got a stamp available but wanted me to write to her to tell her how we were getting on and the money was to buy the stamp.

As we moved away from our home we did not look back. We looked quite respectable in our best clothes and had little or no baggage. Mother didn't want to 'run the gauntlet' under all our neighbours' prying eyes, although it must by now have been obvious to everyone that we were being evicted, so she made us go the 'posh' way round, in the direction of the park instead of the main thoroughfare. She had money in her purse from the sale of our belongings and confidently told us that once we had a place to stay she would find a job and all would be well.

Our first port of call was to a childhood friend of my mother with whom she had kept in contact and who lived far enough away from our 'home' so as not to cause us distress at the sight of someone else occupying it. However the friend was unable to help, her husband would not approve, and it was taking them all their time to keep their own heads above water. Next, we went to another house less well known to us but here again we were turned away. Even then, my mother must have felt that she couldn't face her sister - our aunt Edith, where our brother Jack still lodged.

As darkness fell mother was getting desperate and decided she would knock at the door of some of the grander houses near to aunt Edith and ask for lodgings for the night - showing them that she already had the money to pay for same in her hands. Not surprisingly one by one they turned us away, they were ordinary householders not used to a mother and two children standing on their doorstep asking for shelter.

It was getting late and eventually we sat on a low wall and mother explained to us that because we had not been able to find a place to stay that night we would have to present ourselves at the door of the local union workhouse, who would <u>have</u> to give us shelter for the night. She further explained that it would be better if we went of our own free will because if, instead, we slept on a park bench the N.S.P.C.C. really would have something to 'bite on'. She assured us that it would only be for the one night and that she would find someone to leave us with the next day whilst she went to find a job. It was a big mistake.

Chapter 8

SEPARATION

As we entered the gates of the institution we had no idea that separation was inevitable. It was late at night, we were hungry, and not expected by the people who ran the establishment. Most of the inmates were in bed and mother was trying desperately to convince the reception clerk that she just required an alternative to sleeping rough for the night. We sat in an austere room, each holding a glass of milk and shivered. There was no provision for children here and the best that they could do was to give us a bed for the night, but we would have to be separated. Clifford was taken to the men's section, alone, and mother and I each went to a different ward on the women's section. When we met up again the following morning we were to relate to each other what particular horrors we had endured during the night.

Before all three of us were re-united however, early the next morning mother found me sitting next to the bed in which I had slept, surrounded by wailing women, and she had brought me an orange that she had somehow acquired. I was delighted to see her but wondered why she was giving <u>me</u> the orange instead of Clifford, whom she still regarded as her 'baby' and consequently he was usually first in line for everything. I spoke my thoughts out loud and immediately wished I had not, because she started to cry and said that she was giving it to me. The truth was of course that she could not get into the men's section, and so we went to find someone who could bring my brother to us.

This done, we were all given breakfast and mother was interviewed by the day staff. They explained that <u>she</u> could take shelter there but we children would have to go to a children's home until mother had found a place for us to stay. She argued that we had only intended registering for one night, but as we had no fixed address her pleas fell on deaf ears. They could not possibly return us to the same kind of situation we had just left. She even tried to make demands, like she wanted the authorities to know that we had never been ill-treated and therefore were only to be kept for one or two nights, by which time she would be out of there and working. She was genuine enough and the staff were sympathetic but they wanted to get us children off their hands.

Mother did her best to prepare us for the separation, again reiterating that it would only be for a short time and that until we were all together again Clifford and I had to look after each other. She had pleaded with the staff, as they were making arrangements for our departure, to try to keep us together, explaining that we had never before been separated and that we, brother and sister, did everything together. She also tried to prepare us to be 'streetwise' when we got to the home as there would be all sorts of other children there, some of whom would want to take advantage of us if they could.

While the arrangements were being made we were told to wait in the day room. Mother sat on a chair and we stood one each side of her whilst she held our hands and talked to us. We were surrounded by other women, most of whom looked extremely old to us; many of them were laughing and trying to catch our eye, but she told us to ignore them and listen to what she had to say. Suddenly, in the middle of a sentence, I was aware that she had stopped talking and I could hear a very strange noise; it took a moment or two before I realised that it was coming from mother. It reminded me of the air raid warning wail that we had endured during the war, starting with a deep groan, getting louder and louder, eventually filling the room until no other sound could be heard. I will never forget that bereft hopeless cry as she stood up and clung to me. Someone had come to take me away and although the staff did their best to comfort mother it was to no avail and the last time I saw her in that institution she was clinging to Clifford and they were both crying.

I was taken to another austere room where a man was sitting at a table. He looked ill at ease and after telling me to sit on a chair, picked up a pen and began rolling it around in his fingers. He did not speak further and I sat there, hating the world, especially the situation in which I now found myself. Eventually he disturbed my anguished thoughts by asking me if I knew what the time was!

"There's a clock up there." I replied insolently, nodding at the wall opposite.

"I <u>know</u> there's a clock there," he said tightly. "I want to know if you can tell me the time. Do you know how to tell the time?"

"I'm twelve." I said incredulously, still not giving him the answer he was seeking.

"I don't want to know how old you are," he said. "Lots of people can't tell the time."

"Well I can" I replied, even more insolently.

"What time is it then?" he bellowed.

I hated him as well as the world as I told him the correct time.

Afterwards we sat in strained silence until a short time later a well-dressed woman came into the room; she was obviously very annoyed. It was Saturday morning and she had been telephoned at home to report for duty on her day off. Ignoring me she told her colleague that delivering children into care was not her job. He sympathised but told her that as there was a boy waiting in the day room, also to be taken into care, he could not do both, as we were going to separate homes. She reluctantly agreed to take me, as the home I was going to was only one bus ride away.

She did not smile or speak to me once and I was feeling rather wretched as we waited for the bus. Once on the bus she did not sit next to me but opposite, so again no conversation. It was obvious that she was pretending not to be with me and I resented this as I was well behaved and reasonably dressed.

After alighting from the bus we had a short walk to go, down a tree lined road with extremely large gardens fronting large houses. Turning into a long driveway, flanked by large trees I got my first glimpse of the house, which was to be my 'home' from now on. It was built of dark red brick, very high, with an attic window in the apex. I could not see any activity and the late autumn weather did nothing to enhance the surroundings.

Chapter 9

THE PINES

The door to the front of the house, which confronted us as we climbed a short flight of steps, was huge. It was painted black with dark blue and red leaded lights set into the upper half. It was flanked on either side by matching panels of wood and glass, each almost as big again as the door itself. I had never before seen anything as grand, and even my escort was fazed as she attempted to use the heavy iron doorknocker to announce our arrival - it wouldn't budge. Looking around she noticed a bell-pull and grabbing the handle, gave it a tug. I don't think she had come across one before and I certainly hadn't!

The door was opened by a nurse, small in stature and neatly dressed in uniform, complete with cap on the back of her head. She smiled at us and was pleasant enough. I was amazed as she opened the door, revealing another set of doors leading into a large hall. My escort got only as far as the hall before turning to the nurse and thrusting a form into her hands for her to sign, acknowledging receipt of me. She then explained that she was only deputising for the childcare officer, had no more information, and that the staff here at the home would be contacted on Monday morning by her boss. With that she turned on her heels and sped off down the driveway even quicker than we had come up it.

The nurse smiled at me and shepherded me into the nearest room, a very large one elegantly furnished, with an extremely large bay window overlooking the front grounds and driveway that I had just left behind. Everything about the room seemed massive to me, the ceiling was very high, there was a big marble fireplace and large furniture. Just inside, where I now stood, was a sideboard on which the nurse placed a copy of the form she had just signed. She confirmed with me the details thereon and turning to me told me that if I had any money at all I had to give it to her at that point. I had two and a half old pennies - for a stamp - and I definitely did not want to part with it. I desperately wanted someone (anyone) to know my whereabouts and my face must have shown my dilemma, as I clung to the coppers in my pocket, my eyes filling with tears. She pressed me further.

"You've got some money, haven't you?" she asked me gently. I nodded and she held out her hand with a sad smile.

I reluctantly gave her the coppers, at the same time blurting out that the money was for a stamp to let a friend know how I was getting on.

"I still have to take it from you" she explained. "But I'll tell you what I'll do. I will leave it here on the sideboard and later on I'll exchange it for one of my own postage- stamps, perhaps when you have written your letter".

I brightened up and smiled; it was the first act of kindness I had received in days.

Almost immediately we were joined by another, younger nurse, of bigger build and more boisterous. She was wearing a quizzical expression and looking around for my escort, surprised that she had already left. I was informed that her name was Miss Finch and the more senior nurse was Miss Somers.

Miss Finch was instructed to take me to the ablution room and to find a spare coat peg for me to hang my coat, and to show me what to do. I had no idea what the word 'ablution' meant and I followed her down a flight of stone steps into a cellar, with some trepidation.

As we entered the ablution room I was struck by how warm it was. It was well lit by electric light (there being only a tiny window high above us on the outside wall) and obviously heated by the double set of pipes running all the way round the room just above the concreted floor. Underneath the window was a line of sinks, about a dozen, each complete with hot and cold taps. I had never seen so many before. A few held a hand towel on a hook below the bowl. In the room there was also a heavy free-standing coat rack with numbered pegs on either side, already holding several coats and hats. Miss Finch found me one that was not occupied and told me that would be mine - No. 19. This room was directly underneath the large room that I had left moments earlier, and which turned out to be the staff sitting room, off limits to anyone else. The layout of the cellar rooms and passageway was exactly as above.

In place of the entrance with its two sets of doors (above) next to the ablution room was a small utility room complete with shelves containing shoes and Wellington boots and again it was very warm. As we turned and went back along the duplicate hall, to our right was another large room but this one was cold and Miss Finch shivered as we entered, explaining that this room too was normally out of bounds to children as it contained fresh food. The heating in here was turned off to help keep the food fresh and indeed I could see a whole side of bacon sitting on a bacon slicing machine, which was obviously dangerous to children. I had only ever seen these machines in grocery shops before, always operated by the shop owner.

As we progressed through the cellar we came across a couple of toilets and a large laundry room, which in addition to two copper boilers also housed the heating boiler; this was being stoked with coal by two girls aged about eleven, as we entered. They each held a shovel with a long handle and were running in and out of the room next to this one which was almost full to the ceiling (or so it seemed to me) with coal. It had two similar opening windows to the one in the ablution room, and the coal when it was delivered was tipped through into the room below. Shovels and brushes littered the room, and the long handled shovels, which the girls were carrying, were specially shaped to fit into the small opening towards the top of the heating boiler to feed the roaring flames. The heat was fierce and Miss Finch, after throwing a couple of hefty bucketfuls into the opening, closed the door and said it was stoked enough for now.

I was introduced to the girls and my tour of the cellars over we all went upstairs to the ground floor. When we half way up the steps however the girls were sent back down again to wash the coal dust from their hands and faces.

Immediately opposite the cellar steps was a bathroom containing an extra large bath, sink and toilet, and a large medicine cupboard, but what struck me most of all was that the whole front of the room, leading onto the hall, was mainly see-through glass! I was later to discover that this bathroom was for the children only and therefore could be monitored by the staff.

A large kitchen was to the left of the cellar steps and directly over the boiler room. A few more girls were in this area sitting on a large wooden church pew running the full length of the far side of the room, directly underneath a large window, barred with iron. These girls were aged between five and seven or eight. To my right was a farmhouse dresser, the shelves full of cups, saucers, plates and dishes; the drawers below neatly closed. A fire was burning in the grate and there was a large table with a scrubbed top, a few wooden dining chairs and a large wooden tea trolley, the bottom shelf of which was littered with children's books. The top held a cutlery tray and some mugs. Beyond this room, again to the right, and above the coal cellar, was a scullery equipped with two large porcelain sinks with draining boards, a cooker, on the top of which were several heavy black pans, and an exceptionally large refrigerator, the first 'fridge I had ever seen. When asked if I was hungry, I answered affirmatively, whereupon Miss Finch opened the big 'fridge door and suggested cheese. I didn't like cheese and so was offered jam and bread instead. I was also given a large glass of ice cold milk, poured from a huge enamel jug, again a 'first' for me; it was delicious.

The afternoon was spent with the other girls in that kitchen and I was to discover that the ages ranged from five years upwards. Apart from me the eldest was just eleven; I was nearly thirteen. When the home was fully occupied it could accommodate twenty-one girls, seven to each dormitory I was told, but at present there were three spare beds. The two girls who had been in the cellar with me were among the oldest and did their best to fill me in. Both of them also had a younger sister living there. All the children clamoured around me wanting me to hold their hand or sit next to them. I quickly realised that many of the younger ones in particular were illiterate and nearly all the children had been abused and neglected before being taken into care.

As tea-time approached, Miss Somers and Miss Finch both came back into the kitchen and the older girls were told to put a cloth onto the scrubbed kitchen table top and set it ready for us to eat at. One or two of the girls were directed to the scullery and detailed for various jobs. It was a simple meal as everyone had had a cooked lunch - I had not of course, arriving after lunch was over. A large plate of sandwiches was placed either end of the table and half a dozen or so mugs from the tea trolley (referred to as dinner-wagon by the girls) grouped together at one end. The younger children had to stand around the table, with the exception of one who was lame, having been thrown down some stairs by a parent, whilst one or two of the older girls managed to get a seat on one of the wooden kitchen chairs. I was told to sit down.

There was barely enough room for all of us, and quite a lot of jostling occurred. I sat well back in my chair and let the younger children either side of me reach over for a sandwich. Miss Finch entered from the scullery carrying a huge teapot made from aluminium which, because it was full, was very heavy and a smaller handle situated above the spout had to be used to steady it, as well as the normal side handle. She approached the table telling the children to make way and proceeded to pour the ready-milked tea into the mugs. These were passed to the older girls and I duly received one. The tea was not to my liking being lukewarm, milky, and too sweet. I noticed however that only about half a dozen of us were actually given a mug and Miss Finch had left the room. A short time later she came back and instructed us to pass the mugs of tea to the next person along. I had barely touched mine but the younger girl next to me picked it up with both hands and emptied it.

I looked around the table to find that all the children were behaving in the same manner - drinking the tea while it was available. Some of the children had runny noses, the mucus mingling with their food, and hardly any of them were 'pretty' eaters. I was sickened and when Miss Finch again left the room asked one of the older girls why we had to share the mugs.

"There aren't any more" she replied matter-of-factly.

I was sitting opposite the large dresser where there was a whole row of cups with matching saucers displayed, and pointed this out to her.

"Oh we don't use those." she informed me. "Those are just used in the dining room".

"Where is the dining room?" I enquired. "Why are we not in it now?"

"It's next to the staff sitting room down the hall, but you can't get in – it's locked. We don't use that either. Only at Christmas."

I did not have a drink afterwards although the mugs were refilled many times and sent around the table.

After tea we older girls washed the dishes at the scullery sink whilst the staff had their own tea in their sitting room. As we were on our own I was able to help myself to another cup of milk from the 'fridge but I didn't really know if this would be thought to be misbehaviour, and couldn't be sure that someone wouldn't 'snitch' on me. I had earlier witnessed one or two of the younger girls telling inconsequential tales to Miss Finch who had only walked away, saying that she didn't want to hear any tale-telling.

When everything had been tidied away, we all sat around in the kitchen again. I asked should I use the toilet in the bathroom next door or the one downstairs in the cellar. It turned out that the bathroom was out of bounds without a member of staff and we would have to wait for Miss Finch to return before any of us were allowed down into the cellar. Eventually I heard a buzzing noise and everyone looked up to a small wooden box high up on the wall, showing seven or eight little 'windows', with a tiny pendulum behind each one. Each one represented a room of the house which had a 'service bell' and were all named underneath. The top row was for the ground floor and the bottom row for the bedrooms. The pendulum was swinging for the sitting room. An argument broke out between two of the older girls as to who was going to answer it. I ignored it, as did the younger children. Eventually one of the girls picked up a wooden tray from the tea trolley and took it with her to clear the table in the sitting room.

Shortly afterwards Miss Finch returned to the kitchen and asked if anyone needed the toilet, whereupon most of the younger children raised a hand above their head and an older girl was sent with each one, both instructed to 'be quick about it'.

The next thing on the agenda was to get everyone bathed. Miss Finch opened up the bathroom and half filled the bath, pouring a liquid antiseptic in as she did so. All the girls had the same hairstyle, a short bob with the front piece tied back with a ribbon situated on top of the head to prevent the hair falling over the face. One of the older girls was told to collect everyone's hair ribbon, and everyone was to take off their socks. Socks and ribbons were then taken away by the same girl to be washed downstairs in the laundry sink. Another girl was detailed to help dry the younger children once Miss Finch had bathed them; I was also recruited to help. Two children were put in the bath at the same time, seated one behind the other. After the first one was washed, she was lifted out and stood on a chair by Miss Finch, and the helper then dried the child. To hurry things along, I was to scrub the hands, arms and legs of the second child (with a scrubbing brush) in the bath before passing her down to replace the first one, now being towelled dried. Naked children were queuing up outside the bathroom and the kitchen floor was littered with clothes. Approximately ten to twelve children were bathed in this way, (without the bath water being changed) with Miss Finch helping to dry as well, as the bathing was proceeding more quickly than the drying and there was a backlog. As each child was returned to the kitchen they were told to get dressed again. Many of the little ones forgot what they had been wearing that day and arguments broke out.

Eventually the little ones were done and relative peace reigned once more. The half dozen or so bigger girls left were each given various odd jobs to do by Miss Somers who had come into the kitchen to oversee things. The two staff members should have been off duty for part of the time, one during the afternoon and the other in the evening, but as it happened they were having an 'easy day' sharing the duties. The heating boiler had to be re-stoked, the washed hair ribbons ironed dry, clean clothes put out for each child at the bottom of their bed, issued by Miss Somers but distributed by an older girl, and porridge made in the big black pan ready for morning. The girls had obviously done these things many times and were more than happy to show off their prowess to me as I watched. The porridge was made by Miss Finch but she allowed a girl to light the gas cooker under her supervision and also had a couple of girls 'fetching and carrying' for her. I was amazed when she asked for a spoonful of salt to be poured into the porridge - to my knowledge I had never had porridge but I knew it wasn't a savoury dish! After the porridge came the ironing. There were a few odd items hanging on a clothes-airer, attached to the ceiling and operated by a series of ropes and pulleys, in the kitchen, and this was wound down to extract a selection of underwear and the like to be ironed at the same time as the wet ribbons. A folded sheet was placed on the table and the electric iron removed from the top of the tea-trolley and plugged into a socket. I said that I had done lots of ironing for my mother and that I actually liked to iron, so I was given the job. The only snag was that I had never before had hold of an electric iron and had to be shown how to use it by Miss Finch. At first I found it cumbersome as it was much bigger than a 'flat iron' that I had previously been used to, but I soon became accustomed to it.

Whilst we were getting on with our odd jobs Miss Somers had taken the younger children upstairs, and they were put to bed, so downstairs in the kitchen it was even more peaceful.

After checking that all the jobs had been done Miss Finch refilled the bath and told the rest of us girls to take a bath also, two at a time in the bathroom. She detailed the order in which we were to go and I was to be the very last. Being last meant that I would be climbing into the bath water after several other girls, as again the water was not changed, but I consoled myself that at least I would be able to take a bath in private. I was wrong; as soon as I ventured into the now lukewarm water the door opened and in walked Miss Finch.

"Are you alright?" she enquired. "Are you used to having a bath?"

I nodded, at the same time clasping my hands across my front, otherwise not moving.

"Well come on then, get on with it" she said, and I duly did as I was bid.

She remained in the room, leaning against the sink and I realised that I had no other option than to get out of the bath. As I did so I was aware that she was keenly looking at my body and I felt uncomfortable. It did not occur to me of course that she was checking for bruises or any other sign of ill-treatment.

"What's happened there?" she said, pointing in the direction of my chest.

I looked down but couldn't see anything unusual and my face must have shown puzzlement. She approached and bent down to take a better look, peering at a spot just under my left nipple.

"Oh that? That's a birthmark" I said, relieved as she stood up.

"It's a very big one." she muttered, walking away and telling me to get dressed. I was left trying to look at it without a mirror, as there wasn't one in this bathroom.

Once we were all bathed and the bathroom cleaned up we were given biscuits and milk and left on our own for half an hour or so.

I took this opportunity to assure myself of each of the girls' names, there were now about six or seven of us, and asked about their background; how long had they been in the home etc. It transpired that nearly all of them had been there a long time, one even from being a baby, and three or four of the group had younger sisters living there, and brothers in the corresponding boys home. I had been silently worrying about my brother Clifford all day and this brought it home to me that he was very probably in the boys home by now, but I had been told by the girls that it was a long way from this home. None of them had ever been there so had no further information.

I then decided to quiz them about the staff. Were there other nurses and what were they like? All of them started talking at once and eventually I discovered that Miss Somers was not really in charge, as I had thought. The most senior housemother was Miss Norton but she was not there at the moment, as although she normally slept there, this particular week-end was her week-end off duty and she would not be back until Monday night, ready to start her duties first thing Tuesday morning. I asked if she was as nice as the two I had already encountered and was met with guarded replies. I then asked them which housemother they liked the best and they were more forthcoming. One girl preferred Miss Norton to anyone else, one or two others had their favourites, split between Miss Somers and Miss Finch, but suddenly a girl with beautiful copper red hair said that her favourite was Mrs. Roberts.

"Mrs. Who?" I enquired, not quite hearing the name and unsure whether I had misheard the 'Mrs.' bit.

"Mrs. Roberts" she repeated. "She's upstairs but you've not met her yet."

"Why not?" I wondered, and was then informed that she was another housemother who normally slept there and then had a long week-end off but she had been ill for several weeks and confined to her bedroom. From time to time the girls took food up to her, so they were positive that she was still there. Normally Miss Somers and Miss Finch did not sleep there but at their own family home, coming into work on a daily basis, except when the home was short-staffed, as now.

Just before 9 p.m. Miss Somers came into the kitchen and pronounced bed-time for us. I was told that pyjamas had been laid on a bed for me in the top dormitory (on the second floor), and one of the girls detailed to show me the way and where the upstairs toilet was etc. I was to discover that most of the younger children occupied the two dormitories on the first floor, situated directly over the sitting room and dining room, and all but a couple of older girls slept in the second floor one, where I was to go. Each dormitory contained seven beds, all had an iron 'headboard'. Running down the side of the house was an iron fire escape and my bed was situated next to the emergency exit with a 'push-up' bar to open same. I was told that no-one had to touch this door. I also saw that iron bars were on the outside of the windows in this room, as well as the kitchen downstairs.

My thoughts were racing as we undressed and got into our beds. How were my mother and brother faring and how long would I have to stay here where there was absolutely no privacy. I was exhausted actually, not having had much sleep recently, and as the girl in the nearest bed to the door switched off the light (Miss Finch having shouted "lights out") I settled down to go to sleep but my troubled thoughts would not allow me to. A couple of the girls whispered to each other but I preferred to at last have peace and quiet and after a few sorrowful tears did eventually drift off to sleep.

Chapter 10

SETTLING IN

I was awakened the following morning by a loud banging noise, which turned out to be Miss Finch banging on the bottom step of our flight of stairs with a shoe, in order to wake us up. It was still dark outside and once the girl in the bed nearest the door had got up and turned on the room light the banging ceased.

"Everybody up" shouted Miss Finch, "Get dressed and make your beds, then get down here. Quick about it - you've got ten minutes!"

Everyone was half asleep but moving in a robotic manner to get their clothes on, some quicker than others. I struggled a bit with the clothes I had found on my bed replacing my own clothes which I had left there the night before, but was eventually ready to make some beds, which I was told was done by two girls to each bed.

There were strict rules on how to make the beds. Sheets and blankets were tucked under the mattress and the tops turned down as in hospitals. The whole was then covered with a white cotton counterpane, the corners neatly fitted, these were already known to the girls as 'hospital corners'. When the cover had a smoothed out appearance, the whole was completed by placing a pillow at the head, night clothes in a linen pyjama case placed in front of the pillow.

The three or four girls who were about to go downstairs on to the next floor to make more beds, advised me to go with them. We were met at the bottom by Miss Finch and told to make the beds in the two dormitories there. The younger children had apparently gone downstairs after getting dressed. The same procedure applied in these rooms, one or two of the beds needing clean sheets, issued by Miss Finch.

The floors to all the rooms and landings were highly polished and once the bed-making was complete, one or two of us were given a long handled soft sweeping brush and told to gently sweep under each bed (all situated on the perimeter) to remove the overnight dust and fluff. That done another girl was given a small hand-held scrubbing brush with soft bristles and a tin of floor polish. She had to take off her shoes and kneel on a mat and work her way down the centre of the room towards the door, applying the polish in circular movements. Another girl was to follow, in order to work the polish into the floor, with a scrubber, a set of more, harder, bristles, enclosed in a block, covered by a metal plate on which was situated a swivel mechanism housing a broom handle. This could then be operated to work the scrubber any way one desired, by pushing and pulling it, this time standing so to do. The scrubbers were known as 'dummies' by everyone, and I soon came to follow suit. Finally Miss Finch polished the whole (which was quite a large expanse) with a second 'dummy', the bottom of which was covered by a polishing cloth to give a shiny finish to the now polished floor. Again everyone had to work towards the door and not go back into the room once it was finished or a footprint would be left and the whole operation would have to be done again.

Once the three dormitories were completed to satisfaction the doors were closed and attention turned to the two flights of stairs, which were each carpeted. These were then brushed and vacuumed by us girls, again working in teams, the staircase woodwork finally being dusted by the last girl. There was still the landing to be done and this being as large as the hall below, needed two teams working on it at the same time.

Eventually all was finished upstairs and leaving Miss Finch to give the landing floor a final polish we headed downstairs, right down to the ablution room in the cellar to strip off and have a good wash.

Whilst we had been labouring upstairs and working up a sweat, Miss Somers had been supervising the washing of the faces and hands of the younger girls before they lined up in a queue for her to brush and comb their hair, finally tying each girl's hair with a hair ribbon. By now the little ones had left the cellars and assembled in the kitchen, waiting for Miss Somers to give them breakfast. This enabled us to have a more thorough wash at the line of sinks, finishing just in time for Miss Finch who, having completed the work upstairs, arrived in the ablution room ready to do <u>our</u> hair.

By the time we arrived in the kitchen, clean and tidy, we had been up and about for a couple of hours and I was quite hungry. I was rather pleased to see that the younger children had eaten and moved away from the table, thus enabling us to sit and eat our breakfast. We were given the porridge, made the previous evening, with quite a good spoonful of honey to sweeten it; this was my introduction to honey. To my surprise after the porridge came bacon and sausage, complete with slices of bread and I tucked in, even drinking the tea, which fortunately was given to me in a clean mug.

After breakfast and while the staff were eating theirs in the sitting room, two or three of us older girls washed up in the scullery, as before. Two other girls were detailed to stoke the boiler again and a further two sent to the ablution room, along with all the younger ones to supervise them going to the toilet prior to donning coats and hats. I was to discover that all of us would be going to church shortly, it being Sunday morning.

Eventually we were all ready and with the exception of two girls remaining behind to help Miss Somers prepare lunch, we were assembled together in 'crocodile' form and marched down the driveway and onto the tree-lined road I had encountered the previous day, by Miss Finch. The 'crocodile', which was formed by each girl being paired by another in age and size, started with the little ones at the front. I was at the very rear and did not have a partner. Miss Finch led the whole group at a brisk pace, occasionally turning around to see that all was well.

It was approximately twenty minutes walk to church and the journey made me realise that I was now 'different' to other girls of my age. I hated being in the 'crocodile', walking along ordinary roads and being stared at by other children and adults, no doubt also on their way to church. My only previous encounter with a 'crocodile' of children was when I witnessed some boys, dressed entirely in grey and sporting extremely short haircuts, being marched along, near to my previous home. My mother had told me they were from a home for naughty boys.

At the church door we were halted and lectured by Miss Finch on how to behave inside. We were to sit quietly, listen to what the vicar had to say and definitely not to talk to each other. Most of the children nodded their heads in mute compliance but having witnessed some of the younger ones normally unable to keep still for even five minutes, I wondered how this was to be achieved. I had been to church a few times before, usually being sent in a class from primary school, and I knew how boring it could be for a child. I was older now and reasoned that I could sit still for the duration.

It was even more boring than I had imagined. The service was of 'high church' nature, with much chanting and bowing at the altar, not only by the vicar but also by his curate and even the senior choirboys, one or two swinging incense as they stepped in front of the altar. We children were all seated two or three rows from the front, with only a wheelchair bound lady in front of us. One by one the members of the congregation slowly walked to the Communion rail to take the bread and wine, and the children still had to sit quietly through it, having already endured a half-hour sermon, and two or three hymns. Naturally they were restless and books were continually dropped on the floor throughout the service, with a loud bang.

Eventually it was all over and we were shepherded outside by Miss Finch, who herself gave a sigh of relief. One or two of the children were admonished but it was of almost no consequence. We then began the return walk, in the same order as before.

Once inside the driveway leading to the house the children were 'let off the leash' and told to enter the house via the boot and shoe room, which had an outside door, usually kept locked. It had of course been opened in preparation for our return and this enabled us to hang up our coats and wash our hands, prior to climbing the cellar steps into the kitchen. As Miss Finch bounded up the steps ahead of us I could smell a wonderful aroma of roast beef as she opened the connecting door to the kitchen.

The two girls who had been left behind and Miss Somers had obviously been busy preparing lunch whilst we had been away. The table was set with cutlery and we bigger girls were detailed to serve the younger ones first. The plates were set out in a row in the scullery and the food placed on them in a regimented manner by both Miss Somers and Miss Finch, finally the mashed potato and beef and vegetables being given a ladleful of gravy. After serving the younger ones, we were told that we could either make room for ourselves at the kitchen table or stand here in the scullery at the worktop to eat our food. I chose the scullery.

I thoroughly enjoyed my lunch, it was exactly to my liking and I was hungry. The main course was followed by sponge pudding with custard, and it all reminded me of how things used to be when my father was alive and we all ate together the tasty meals cooked by my mother.

The staff went off to have their meal, the same as ours, and we older girls all got down to work on the washing up of the dishes and pans. All the girls knew the order in which things were done efficiently and in a relaxed way got on with it, talking and laughing together. I was more serious, only half-listening to their chatter. My thoughts were of my mother and brother.

Later, when children and staff alike had finished lunch and everything had been cleared away, everyone again assembled in the ablution room for outdoor clothes. This time we were all to go to Sunday school in the church hall. I could hardly believe it! Surely I didn't have to make the same 'crocodile' journey again. I did, but this time a few of the more unruly little ones were kept behind, the rest each being allocated to an older girl who was to be responsible for that particular child while we were on the road. We were to proceed as before in a column of pairs, headed by the girl with the beautiful copper coloured hair and her partner, and I was to bring up the rear making sure no-one dropped out of line.

Of course the children were not obedient once we had left the grounds, and there was a considerable amount of stopping and talking on the way. Eventually we arrived at the school hall and Margaret - the girl with the lovely hair - who knew which class all the children were in, sent them to their destination. She indicated that I should go with her, and we sat informally in a class of about eight or ten children, not all of whom were from the home. The majority came from ordinary family backgrounds.

Sunday school over, we eventually marched back to the home, entered by the same entrance as at morning, and once more ascended the steps to the kitchen, to a nice warm fire.

Whilst we were thus, just hanging around in the kitchen amid a hubbub of chatter, the main kitchen door was opened and all heads were turned in that direction, with a moment of silence prevailing. The next thing I knew, all the children were moving towards the door, crying out with pleasure. Standing in the doorway was a lady wearing a dress and cardigan, looking very frail and as if she had lost much weight.

Margaret was the first to reach her and with a delighted smile flung her arms around her to hug her.

"Hello copper knob" she smiled back, ruffling Margaret's hair, as she tried to greet all the children. "Don't knock me down will you? Let me come in and have a seat."

The children made way and she sat by the fire, her gaze coming to rest on me.

"And you must be Mavis" she said, smiling at me.

Everyone was talking at once, asking questions and showing her books and the like.

Margaret asked if she was coming back to work.

"Not just yet" she replied. "Another week or two."

Margaret was disappointed; this was her favourite housemother, Mrs. Roberts.

She again addressed me, asking how I was getting on, had I settled in?

Of course I replied that I was doing alright, not volunteering that what I really wanted was to be with my mother and brother, and there really wasn't much point to settling in for me, as I was only here for a few days. I didn't belong here.

I didn't know it then but this kind and gentle woman was to play a very big part in the rest of my life, helping me to overcome many heartaches, guiding me along the right path into adulthood. I owe her an enormous debt of gratitude.

Chapter 11

BACK TO SCHOOL

The rest of that Sunday afternoon and evening were spent in much the same way as the previous day, with absolutely no privacy. The kitchen in which we had to stay was sparsely furnished with only the church pew and a few chairs available for us to sit on, all of which were not very comfortable. The walls were completely tiled from top to bottom with a sickly green square tile and a large clock was mounted on one wall. The floor was covered with quarry tiles. It soon became apparent to me that hardly any of the children could tell the time and even most of the bigger girls only took a guess at it. I had nothing to occupy me, the books lying around only suitable for young children and all were in a state of neglect. The other girls talked with each other and defended their siblings when necessary.

We were all in bed early that night, in preparation for school the next day, and I was quite relieved to finally get some time to dwell on my predicament. Miss Somers had earlier asked me where I had been going to school but I had not been forthcoming, saying only that I had not attended for a long time.

The next morning we were again woken early, this time Miss Finch entering the room and switching the light on and off several times. Everyone except me had clean clothes at the foot of their bed and were told to get dressed, after which we made the beds and went on to the other two dormitories. Each girl was supplied with a black pinafore-type apron, complete with ties to fit around the waist, to protect their school clothes, as we did our cleaning. On entering these lower dormitories I was surprised to find one set of beds moved from the perimeter of the room to the centre. This section was then polished in exactly the same way as we had polished the centre of the room the previous day. The beds were then carried - in order not to mark the now polished floor - by us and gently lowered to their previous positions. The other side of the room was then attacked in exactly the same way, finally finishing up polishing the centre. I was to discover that Sunday had been treated as a 'day of rest' and the cleaning duties relaxed as much as possible.

All three dormitories were cleaned in the same manner, after which we went downstairs to have our wash and brush-up and eat breakfast. Apparently a cleaning lady came every week-day to help the staff with the cleaning duties of the rest of the house. The landing and downstairs hall, both identical to each other, would be done later on that morning.

All the children attended a local infant and junior school and the staff kept an eye on the clock as they endeavoured to make sure each girl was ready by 8.30 a.m. I was too old to go to this school and was told to help in any way that I could and that I would be dealt with later. Finally everyone was ready and assembled outside, towards the back entrance of the house. They were then joined by Miss Finch who once more took them in a 'crocodile' manner, out of a large back gate which I had not noticed before, and which entered a lane running parallel with the tree-lined road at the front

of the house. The lane led to a main road which had to be crossed in order to get to the school.

After delivering the children safely to school Miss Finch returned and the two members of staff had their own breakfast at the kitchen table. A cup of tea was offered to the cleaning lady who had by now arrived and eventually, after I had made a start on the huge pile of dishes to be washed, one was offered to me, which I gladly accepted, this being taken in a cup and saucer with milk and sugar added instead of the lukewarm ready-milked tea offered at breakfast.

This was an opportunity for both Miss Somers and Miss Finch to find out more about where I had been to school and I was forced to tell them the name of the school I had last attended. Miss Somers then said that I would not be going to school that day until

she had made some enquiries about me and that I could help with the cleaning.

The rest of the morning was spent doing just that, and I was kept busy the whole time.

This suited me as at least I was not 'imprisoned' in the kitchen, and even discovered more rooms which I had not until then had cause to enter. Miss Somers had been occupying a staff bedroom just opposite to the two lower dormitories, but would not be sleeping there that night as

Miss Norton would be returning, ready to start work the following day - Miss Somers would be taking the day off. The room had to be thoroughly cleaned including of course a change of bed linen and it was quite a revelation to me to see what luxury was contained in this room. Nicely furnished and carpeted, with mirrored wardrobes and dressing tables, and homely photographs and pictures scattered about. The staff bathroom was just at the end of the landing.

Up the flight of stairs to my dormitory and then along a further landing was the attic room I had noticed from outside when I arrived. This was where Miss Finch had been sleeping for the past two nights. It was not really a bedroom but meant to be a playroom for the children. Stored inside however were spare mattresses and Miss Finch had made a bed for herself on top of two or three of these instead of travelling to and from work on her bicycle. Also in this room as well as toys and games was a very large dolls house, complete with furniture. As I helped her to tidy the room up she told me that this room was out of bounds without a member of staff. I noticed that the room also contained a sewing machine, used to repair torn clothes etc., and that the tiny window in this room also, was barred with iron, this time on the inside.

Back down the small landing on this floor, and next to my dormitory, was another door, locked. We entered once Miss Finch had used one of her keys hanging from a small chain attached to the belt of her nurses uniform. This was known as the store-room, containing all domestic linen as well as clothes for the children, neatly stacked on shelves with sliding cupboard doors. After she had put her blankets away (having first put the bed-linen into a laundry basket) she attempted to find more clothes to fit me, as I had not yet had a change of attire. She was not very successful but did manage to find different socks and shoes for me, as well as underwear, which just about fitted. I hated the shoes and was sorry that they fitted; they were of brown leather, lace-up brogue type. I asked why I couldn't wear my own clothes that I had arrived in, as these had been my best ones. She replied that as yet they had not been laundered and in any case would be kept in this store room, ready for me to go home in once they had been. This satisfied me, as at least there was now a possibility that I would be getting out of there shortly.

Eventually our cleaning duties took us down to the ground floor and here with Mrs. Lee, the cleaning lady, I was to discover the dining room, as she opened the door to dust and lightly polish inside. I was amazed. It was a very high large room, similar to the sitting room next to it, complete with fireplace, this time with a wooden surround and high mirror. Arranged around the room were tables and chairs to seat four people at each, six tables in all. Just in front of the bay window was a larger oblong table for serving purposes. Each table was fitted with a tablecloth, suitably waterproof for spillages and able to be kept clean with a wet cloth. In the centre of each table was a small pot of ever-lasting flowers. She swept the floor with a soft brush and Miss Finch finished it off with a polishing from the 'dummy'. I noticed that the door to this room was left ajar for the time being.

As lunchtime approached I could smell the wonderful aroma of cooking and I realised that I was rather hungry and ready for a rest from cleaning. There was much bustling about from the staff, with a sense of urgency prevailing. The sitting room table was set for dining for three people, as Matron would be arriving shortly I was told. I was to eat in the kitchen with Mrs. Lee. The hall had been given a final polish and we all awaited Matron's arrival. After a short wait we heard the engine of a car, witnessed the parking of it, underneath the kitchen window, followed by the ringing of the front door bell. Miss Somers who had been waiting in the sitting room after cooking the lunchtime meal let her in.

Again the meal was excellent and I readily ate my portion, accompanying it with a glass of water. Pudding was served and eaten, the staff, including Matron, retiring to the sitting room for a short while. Mrs. Lee had a doze and I made a start on the washing up after being told to do so by Miss Finch, who had cleared the table herself on this occasion. Matron then went on her round of inspecting the dormitories and rooms. Before leaving she came into the kitchen but didn't speak to me. She had a matronly figure and was dressed in tweed outdoor clothes complete with hat, and she, I noticed, also had brogues on her feet. Both Miss Somers and Miss Finch heaved a sigh of relief as the car moved off down the driveway. This inspection then was what all the cleaning fuss was about earlier, and I was to discover that Matron came for lunch almost every weekday.

Unfortunately Matron, not having yet been into the offices of the childcare unit that day, was not able to give Miss Somers any further details regarding me, but apparently she intended to telephone later on, when she had made enquiries. Arriving into care on Friday night as we did seemed to have upset the system somewhat.

The rest of the day was spent doing odd jobs, such as polishing the cutlery kept in the dining room and again helping Mrs. Lee, especially with the ironing, as I was able to do this unsupervised now. The children came home in twos and threes, having first been escorted across the road at the top of the lane by Miss Finch who had gone out to meet them. Tea was served to the children; the meal that day being cooked cheese and tomato bake accompanied by toast which had been made by me, having first been shown how to operate the toaster - again I had not seen one before. I did not like either cheese or tomato and managed to get away with eating just the toast. As it happened I was not particularly hungry, having eaten a good lunch.

All the same procedures were adopted for the bath and bedtime routines with clean clothes again being issued where necessary. My clothes were taken away by Miss Somers and given a brush and press to make me presentable in case I went to school the following day. Once we had all been bathed Miss Finch collected her coat and mounted her bicycle to go home for the night. Miss Somers would wait until Miss Norton arrived for duty and then she too would go home, by bus.

Matron mustn't have come forth with instructions about what to do with me, because as I went to bed that night Miss Somers admitted that she did not know what was to happen the next day as far as I was concerned. I would see Miss Norton the following morning and she would be totally in charge. Miss Finch would be coming in to assist her. I fell asleep not sure what to expect but aware that both children and staff were careful not to put a foot wrong when Miss Norton was around.

* * *

The normal routine was adopted the next day, with Miss Norton coming into our dormitory to wake us. By the time we were hard at work with the dummies, cleaning and polishing the floors Miss Norton had disappeared; so had a girl named Mary, one of the older girls. Mary did not sleep in our dormitory but in one of the lower ones, directly opposite Miss Norton's room, and so it was some time before I missed her. I asked one of the other girls where Mary was and with a furtive look at the door she whispered to me that she would probably be in Miss Norton's room, as she was her 'pet'.

"What is she doing in there?" I asked.

"Most likely reporting everything that has been happening over the week-end" she replied.

Actually she was also having a cup of tea from the tray sent up for Miss Norton. I witnessed this for myself, the door to the room being ajar, as I downed tools and made my way to the toilet. I could easily see the unfairness of this, new as I was to procedure. I would have loved to have a cup of tea myself, but no such luck. The act did however corroborate for me what the other girls already knew, Mary was the 'mole' and to be treated with caution. It also explained why they had been so reticent on my first evening, when I had asked them about the staff, and Mary was present, in fact she was the one who had preferred Miss Norton.

Eventually the upstairs work was done, and as it was a week-day a sense of urgency prevailed, and we were told to get downstairs and get ready for school. Mary was already in the ablution room as we arrived there, and even I could see that she had a smirk on her face. The other girls ignored her, but eventually we all went upstairs to the kitchen together, to have breakfast. Miss Finch was on duty in the kitchen and bid us 'good morning', placing mugs in front of us and organising the distribution of dishes of porridge. Again the younger children had already eaten and we were each given our own mug.

Miss Norton entered the kitchen just as we were finishing our breakfast and I saw that in addition to her uniform she was now wearing a peculiar head-dress, rather like a large folded handkerchief, placed on her head in the manner of a nun's habitual headgear, held in place by two hair clips. It was white and fell over her shoulders, part way down her back, her grey hair just visible in one or two places at the front.

She made a beeline for me, told me to stand up and asked me which school I attended. Having already told Miss Somers the previous day, I had no alternative other than to repeat the name of my school, adding that I had not been to school for a long time.

"Well that's where you will be going today", she said in a determined voice. "Do you think you can find your own way there from here?"

I was appalled, I hardly knew my way to the main road, let alone my old school, which, I felt sure, was some distance away. I had noticed however when I was being brought by bus to the home, that we had passed my lovely library, where I had spent many happy hours with my friend June when I was younger. At the time, on the bus, I had wondered if I would ever again get a chance to go there, and I had mentally noted it as a landmark.

"I know my way to school from the library" I volunteered.

"So if someone took you to the library, could you then find your way to school and back here again?" she queried.

I nodded, not trusting myself to speak further. I was panicking at the thought of having to go back to school - to an unknown teacher - and to face all my former friends and neighbours.

"Right. It's eight-o-clock now. If I take you to the library straight away, you will have an hour to get to school on time. That should be enough", she said. She had previously worked out the approximate distance when I gave her the name of the school.

After telling Miss Finch that she would be back in time for her to take the other girls to school, she flung a black serge cape over her shoulders, setting her 'kerchief straight at the same time and instructed me to get downstairs and get my coat and to join her at the back gate.

I felt very miserable as I did as I was told. I did not like the idea of walking along the main road to the library accompanied by this authoritative woman, wearing such headgear. Furthermore I could guess that my own head didn't look good, as she had struggled earlier that morning to tie a ribbon on my over-long hair and had eventually given up in disgust saying that I would have to get my hair cut. I had not been able to see the finished result, there being no mirror, but I felt stupid all the same. I vowed to take the ribbon off as soon as I left her. Even my clothes looked odd and didn't fit me well.

Half way up the lane she remembered that I would need feeding at lunch time and did not have any dinner money. Telling me to wait for her at the top of the lane she went back to get some and I waited until she joined me. Fortunately it was early and no other children were about while I waited.

Once at the library I made it obvious that I knew my way from there and I was able to give her the names of some of the roads I would be travelling down. Making sure I also knew my way home and after giving me money for school dinners, she left me, going back the way we had come.

I dreaded the day ahead, but carried on in the direction of school, knowing now that it would take me quite some time to get there and aware that if I really <u>had</u> to go to school and face the teachers I hardly knew, it would be better if I arrived on time. Somewhere along the way I pulled off the ribbon, but as I had no comb my hair then looked long and unkempt.

I had to go through the district where my mother had knocked on doors asking for lodgings, which only added to my misery. I then had to cross the park where we had considered sleeping rough, eventually arriving at the red-brick-built school I had briefly attended in my 'other life'.

Other pupils were arriving by the time I got there and eventually one of them recognised me, laughing at my turning up out of the blue, asking did I know which class I would be in. Of course I had no idea and dreaded the thought of knocking on the door of the headmaster's study to ask if I could come back to school, as I had been told to do by Miss Norton.

I hung around in the playground, trying to keep out of sight of my contemporaries and with the exception of a few astonished previous classmates who nodded a brief greeting, I managed to do this, and enter school at the sound of the bell. I then reluctantly made my way to the headmaster's study, only to find that the door was not in the same place as before, a few alterations having taken place. However I sat on a chair outside the door and waited for someone to see me.

Fortunately for me I was spotted and recognised by Miss Murphy, who had taught me right at the beginning of my attendance at this school when I was heading the leaderboard with excellence, two or three years previously. Telling me to wait there she carried on to her classroom to organise her class into assembly and then came back to talk to me.

I tried to hide the fact that I was in a children's home but she probably guessed with my vague answers to her questions and she did not probe further. She explained that the headmaster was off sick, and after asking me to confirm my age, she then took me to a class containing most of the children from the neighbourhood I had just left, and had a quiet word with the teacher. Unfortunately this teacher didn't take kindly to another child turning up in the middle of a lesson and after telling me to sit down, ignored me. I had always been scared of this particular teacher, having heard many stories from my brother Jack and other older pupils about her short temper and sarcasm.

After the mid-morning break, during which I had had to answer various curious questions from my former classmates, we had no sooner sat down at our desks than Mrs. Eaves, the class teacher, stood in front of the central blackboard facing us.

"Right." she said. "I'm sure that you'll all remember from last week when we talked about spiral staircases." There was a murmur of agreement.

"Can anyone now tell me what a spiral staircase is?" she queried.

A few hands, including mine, shot up.

"You." she said, pointing in my direction. "Tell us what it is."

In a flash my thoughts were back at my old home, listening in rapt attention to my brother Jack a few years earlier, telling me about his new teacher. He had asked me then to describe what a spiral staircase was and when I had used my forefinger to make a corkscrew movement in mid air, he had burst out laughing, explaining that nearly everybody did the same when trying to describe one - Mrs. Eaves had told him. He advised me to try to remember it when I found myself in her class. I had remembered it just in time.

Clasping my hands firmly in front of me on the desk I had to think quickly.

"It's a staircase that goes round and round, at the same time that it's going up." I declared, further pressing my hands together.

There were gasps, groans and titters from the rest of the class, most of whom were sitting behind me, but I continued to look at the teacher as I answered.

"Somebody's told you!" she almost screamed at me. "Who's let the cat out of the bag?" she demanded, looking furiously at the rest.

Everyone denied it of course and she eventually had to accept the cries of innocence.

I did not enlighten her as she told me it was a rare event for a person describing such a staircase not to add a 'pictorial' description with their hands.

Giving the rest of the class work to do she then told me to approach her desk as I had no books of any kind.

"I suppose I'd better put you in the register first." she announced in a tight voice.

I had obviously not done myself any favours not allowing her to prove a point to the class and her manner towards me was cool.

I gave her my name when she requested it, but had no idea of the address I was now living at.

"What?" she exclaimed in a loud voice. "You don't know where you live? How old are you?

I was aware of the other pupils covertly watching, and my face was by now scarlet as I answered her.

"Have you no idea at all?" she asked incredulously. " What part of town do you live in, is it near to this school?"

Remembering the library I made a stab at that district, giving the name, but secretly not believing this was correct.

"And what about the road? Can you tell me that?"

I remembered the name of the lane where I had waited that morning for Miss Norton.

"Waverley Road" I said.

She had not heard of this road, which was not surprising since it was a private unadopted road leading only to the back entrances of a few large houses.

"Do you have any brothers or sisters?" she asked me. I nodded.

"Do <u>they</u> know where they live?" She continued.

I explained that they didn't live with me.

"Whom do <u>you</u> live with then?" she further questioned.

"A lady" I mumbled, my eyes filling with tears.

"Well see if you can get this <u>lady</u> to tell you your correct address by tomorrow." she said. "I presume you <u>will</u> be coming to school tomorrow?" I nodded.

She must have grown tired of questioning me at this point, because getting down from her high desk-chair, and telling me to 'speak up for goodness sake' she moved across the room to find books and pencils etc. for me, further instructing me to follow the lessons as best I could.

* * *

Lunchtime came and the class filed out to get coats from the cloakroom. Some pupils went home, others went to designated school dinner places in the hall. There were two sittings.

Not knowing what to do and not having had the courage to mention school meals to Mrs. Eaves, I donned my coat. Feeling the money in my pocket I decided I would go to a local pastry shop where in the past my mother had sent me to buy hot pies. It was a fair distance away but I knew the way and knew also that I could make it there and back before afternoon class. I hoped it would be open - it was of course, catering for the school pupils as well as the local mill workers.

The lady in the shop was quite surprised when I offered the half-crown I had, as payment, but I made sure she gave me the correct change, having first verified the price of the pie from a display board. I stood on the pavement outside the shop and quickly ate it, deciding I needed another! I looked longingly at the display of drinks for sale, whilst queuing for my second pie, but as they seemed very expensive, I decided not to push my luck, as the money I had would probably have to last me for the rest of the week. I would have a drink of water when I got back to school.

I got back to school in time without having to answer any more questions from fellow pupils; I was careful to avoid meeting them. I had a quick drink in my cupped hands in the cloakroom and went into class. Nobody bothered me and the rest of the afternoon was spent doing lessons.

At the end of the school day, along with everyone else I made my way to the exit, having first collected my coat. Here I <u>was</u> questioned by the others who wanted to know whom I was living with and which way I was going home. I told them I was living with my aunt who lived across the park, and that I would have to go, she would be waiting for me. I indicated which way I would be going, knowing full well that the majority of the others went the opposite way. I set off, leaving them in a group staring after me.

I was thoroughly dejected as I made my way back to the home. I had had a miserable day, dusk was falling, and it was a lonely journey with nothing to look forward to at the end of it. Added to this I knew that I was not entirely sure of the way back.

It was almost dark by the time I showed up and Miss Norton greeted me furiously once I entered the kitchen.

"Where have you been?" She demanded.

"Coming back". I answered truthfully.

"It can't possibly have taken you all this time to get back", she growled. "How long did it take you to get to school this morning? Were you late?"

I replied that I had not been late and that I had also come straight back. It took that much time to do so. I did not think to tell her that the majority of the journey back was up a steep hill, followed by another, not quite as steep. This had obviously slowed my progress, whereas it had all been downhill on my way there.

By now the other children had already eaten and my meal was plated up in the oven.

After telling me to sit down she retrieved it and placed it in front of me. My heart sank - it was fish pie, complete with white savoury sauce, which by now had congealed. I really hated it and attempted to leave it uneaten, but she was having none of it, telling me it was good for me. I struggled on but it was obvious that we would be there all night if she watched over me. In the end she went off to have her own meal and I dumped it. Later she was to enquire how I had got on with the school dinner money and I truthfully told her how I couldn't find out how to register for school meals and so I had bought two pies. She took away the change.

When I eventually climbed into bed that night I felt really sorry for myself but there was no-one to whom I could unload my woes so I just hid under the blanket and wept, worried that Clifford who was much younger than me could be faring even worse. Most of all I missed my mother.

Chapter 12

MRS. ROBERTS

As the week progressed I learned to adjust to my surroundings. On my second day at School I was able to present Mrs. Eaves with my address, having managed to catch Miss Somers between jobs on her return to work that morning, and once I had explained to her what I needed, she wrote it down for me on a scrap of paper, showing that "The Pines" was the name of the home, followed by the address, and incorporating the information that it was a children's home.

I knew that I would have to hand the address to Mrs. Eaves on arrival in class and attempted to do so immediately after the register had been called. She was busy and told me to leave it on her desk and I was thankful to do so. I hoped she would not inform the rest of the class. Miss Norton again gave me money for school dinners, but when I returned in the evening having once again bought my lunch she said that she would telephone the school the following day. The next morning Mrs. Eaves called me to her desk and said that school dinners had now been arranged for me and I would be at the first sitting.

I plodded on with the lessons as best I could, being aware that I had fallen far behind my fellow pupils. However I knew that I had the advantage of being brighter than many of them and set myself to work to catch up. I genuinely enjoyed learning.

Almost every day I was questioned by at least one of my contemporaries about my 'aunt' and at least one girl commented on my appearance, saying that I looked much tidier now that I was living with my aunt. She meant no harm so I agreed, also mentioning that I didn't really like the clothes I now wore. I had been kitted out with a skirt and tunic type jacket - a bit austere I thought, but she was right I did look clean and tidy. By now I had learned to keep the hair ribbon in place as Miss Somers had told me it was obligatory - she was sorry!

* * *

Saturday arrived and I was still no nearer to finding anything out about my mother and brother. It was now a week since we had been separated and already several days longer than I had anticipated, my mother having told me it was just for a night or two.

I dreaded the weekend feeling that I would be cooped up in the kitchen and have to attend church again on Sunday.

I was right to feel apprehensive. After breakfast on Saturday Miss Norton told us all to line-up outside the bathroom. There was an instant groan from the children, as they knew what was coming, but everyone complied. She then proceeded to give every girl a spoonful of cod liver oil, delivered from the same spoon. I noticed that Mary was first. I had no option other than to swallow it quickly as advised but I almost brought my breakfast back! No sooner had she replaced the huge bottle of the stuff back into the medicine cabinet than she was ordering everyone to line-up again. This time we were each given a measure of a liquid laxative, which wasn't too bad, reminding me of the syrup of figs my mother used to give me. At least it helped to take the taste of the fish oil away. Apparently Mary did not like this so was given a mint concoction instead! This ritual was repeated every Saturday morning.

I was right about being confined to the kitchen. It was raining outside and eventually there was a steady stream of children going to the toilet anyway. The bigger girls were given a few jobs to do; stoke the boiler, fill the coal-scuttles for kitchen and sitting room, peel potatoes ready for lunch, wash a few odd items in the laundry room and polish all shoes ready for church the next day. The morning wore on.

After lunch it turned out that all the girls were to have their hair cut. Apparently a hairdresser came once a month to do this. Her name was Eileen and she worked at a local salon. She was doing this extra job in her own time, at Miss Norton's request, an average of eighteen to twenty haircuts, all the same, short bob, with the front piece tied back with a ribbon.

It was a welcome distraction for most of the girls, especially the younger ones who could run around unsupervised in the ablution room where the cutting took place.

Eileen did her best to keep them in order, but they were able to let off steam down there and took full advantage of the situation. One by one we bigger girls drifted in, after finishing the washing-up etc. to have our hair cut. When it came to my turn and I reluctantly stood in front of her, I pleaded with Eileen not to cut mine, as I was too old to have my hair done in the same childish fashion and in any case I would be leaving there shortly. She was apologetic but firm, saying that she was sorry, but she had particularly been instructed to cut mine, in fact she wasn't really due until next Saturday but had been called in a week early in order to make sure I had it cut. I was very crestfallen and she tried to console me by telling me she would make it look as good as possible.

I was near to tears when I saw the long cuttings of hair falling around me to the floor. The whole procedure seemed endless and I had no way of checking the outcome, there was no mirror anywhere for us girls. In the end, when she had finally finished, she held her own hand-mirror for me to look into and I let the tears fall. She pointed out that she had not renewed my hair-ribbon and maybe the staff would let me go to school with my hair clipped back with the hairclip she had just produced, instead of a ribbon; that wouldn't look so bad, would it? I was too upset to reply.

* * *

Later on that afternoon Miss Somers handed a cup of tea to Margaret telling her to take it up to Mrs. Roberts who was in her room, and turning to me told me to go as well. Margaret was delighted and carefully carried the tea-cup balanced on a saucer up the first flight of stairs. The room was immediately at the top on the left, and Margaret stood outside, telling me to knock on the door. We then entered, after being requested to do so.

This room was much smaller than Miss Norton's but extremely cosy. It contained a mirrored dressing table, large wardrobe and bits of occasional furniture, as well as the bed. Lots of personal belongings were lying around. Mrs. Roberts was sitting on a chair by the window and after greeting and thanking us for the tea with a warm smile, told us to sit on the bed where she could see us. Margaret was quite excited to be in the room with this friendly housemother, and quite talkative. I sat quietly.

"I can see you've had your hair cut Copperknob" she smiled, nodding at Margaret's head. "It's beautiful as usual, and that's a nice green ribbon you're wearing".

Margaret beamed.

Turning to me she said "And what about yours Mavis, do you like it?" I didn't answer. Margaret informed her that I didn't.

"What don't you like about it?" she asked me.

"It's too short and I didn't want it cutting". I answered. I had seen my reflection in the mirror of the dressing table as we entered and was not happy.

"Well it's nicely cut, and I see you have a hairclip holding it back", she said. I just sat there despondently.

Then: "Margaret look in my haberdashery drawer, I think you'll find a hair slide in there." she said.

I had never heard the word 'haberdashery' before, but Margaret jumped up eagerly and rummaged about in a top drawer of the dressing table, she was obviously familiar with this room. She brought out a small pink hair slide.

"No, there's a better one than that." Mrs. Roberts chided, chuckling.

Margaret eventually brought out a black hair slide shaped like a butterfly, decorated with bits of gold coloured beads. By this time the drawer was in disarray and wouldn't close but Mrs. Roberts ignored it.

"Come here" she said to me. I slid off the bed.

Asking Margaret to pass her a hairbrush from the dressing table and telling me to kneel in front of her, she proceeded to brush my hair and insert the hair slide in place of the clip. Getting up to inspect it in the mirror, I realised that she had somehow, by re-arranging the hair slide, given my hair a softer style. I was grateful but still subdued. I still didn't like it.

"It'll soon grow", she said quietly, by way of comfort.

After a short time Miss Somers entered the room, collected the now empty tea cup and asked Margaret to help her sort out some odd-jobs downstairs. Margaret was obviously disappointed at this, and reluctantly left the room. I had made a move to leave as well but Miss Somers insisted I stayed where I was and kept Mrs. Roberts company for a while. With hindsight I can see that the whole episode was contrived, but at the time it was deftly done.

We chatted, and bit by bit this caring woman got to know a little of my background and how upset I was at being separated from my mother and brother.

"Well, I can probably make enquiries about your brother" she offered "And I may even be able to find out how your mother is going on as well. But it will take a few days". My eyes shone.

"In the meantime try to come back from school a little bit quicker, will you?" The other staff think you take too long. You're coming back in the dark!"

"But I <u>do</u> come straight back" I objected. "It's a long way."

After asking how I was going on at school and if I had any problems, she sympathised with me about my short hair-cut and how everyone would laugh at me at school, saying that I had to be strong - "sticks and stones and all that!" Telling me once again that it would soon grow.

As I left the room at her bidding to go downstairs for tea, I consoled myself, not for the first time that I wouldn't be staying long. Another week and I would be out of there!

The rest of the week-end was spent in much the same way as the previous one but instead of the friendly Miss Finch taking us to church, we were led there in the 'crocodile' at a brisk pace by Miss Norton accompanied at the front by Mary, and nobody spoke. On arrival at church I discovered that Miss Norton enjoyed greeting and chatting to the rest of the congregation, even genuflecting before taking her seat in the pew (something I had never witnessed before) and taking communion. The children, though restless, did not cause too much disruption. Miss Norton insisted I wore a hair ribbon like the rest.

* * *

I endured the first day of the following week back at school, complete with new hair-cut and ribbon, and surprisingly I was not made fun of as much as I had feared. Just a bit of teasing from one or two pupils undoing the ribbon from the rear etc. I had the hair slide in my coat pocket as I had fully intended to remove the ribbon on my journey there and replace it with the hair slide but knew I couldn't lie to Miss Norton, saying that it had fallen off, with any conviction. She had made sure it was a tight fit that morning, and I couldn't manage to put it back myself.

The next day when she was doing my hair Miss Norton picked up a ribbon as usual and then putting her hands on my shoulders turned me around to face her.

"I believe that you don't like wearing a hair ribbon", she said, a bit sarcastically. I shook my head apprehensively. "Mrs. Roberts has given you a hair-slide hasn't she?" she continued. I nodded.

"Where is it?"

I indicated the coat rack nearby. "In my pocket" I answered.

"Well get it then and put it in" she commanded. I did the best I could without mirror.

She hardly looked at me.

"Now then" she said. "From today you will be going to school by bus. There will be one passing the bottom of the road at 8.30, do you know how to get there?"

To get the bus at the <u>bottom</u> of the by now familiar tree-lined road fronting the house, I knew I would have to walk even further than when we walked to church, but in the same general direction. I had never been down to the bottom of this road, having used a different bus route when first arriving at the home, alighting at the top of the road. It was a long road.

"I think so" I replied.

"You will also come back the same way," she announced. "I will give you the bus fare."

After breakfast as I made my way down the road I was grateful that I had once again managed to get hold of Miss Somers before setting off and she had given me one or two landmarks to look for, and I made it to the bus stop on time. I realised that this road I had now reached was the one that my mother and I had travelled along many times on our way to the cemetery; we had gone by tram. However I now waited at the unfamiliar bus stop as instructed and ignored the tram, which came lumbering down the road in the direction of my old home. It stopped at a tram stop a little way down the road and I didn't dare to go after it in case I missed it and the bus came and I missed that as well. I had never been on a bus by myself before and was a bit apprehensive, but when it arrived and I got on, I gave the conductor my fare just as I would have done on the tram and all went well. I sat just inside the bus near to the exit as I wasn't too sure where it would stop near to school.

As the bus progressed down the road, having overtaken the tram, I saw many familiar landmarks and knew that we were approaching my old home, recognising the street signs and shops. There were people I knew waiting at the tram stop but no-one was looking at the bus as it carried on past them to the bus stop situated further along the road. The bus fare was twice the price of the tram fare and so was shunned by 'my people' only normally being used when the destination was one where trams did not run . We eventually arrived near to school and I alighted, in plenty of time for the school bell.

In the evening returning from school meant that I had now to walk the opposite way from the route I had been taking the previous week, back down to the main road to catch the bus, in the direction once again of my old home. Of course this caused surprise with my old neighbours who wanted to know where I was going as they accompanied me out of school, when I turned in the direction of my old home to walk with them. I told them my aunt wanted me to catch the bus as it was dark when I got home if I walked it. In response to their incredulous cries about using the bus instead of the tram, I told them it was quicker.

I had seriously thought about substituting the tram for the bus and thus saving myself half the fare but I wasn't sure that I would recognise the road where I was to alight, it being in a different place from the bus stop, and if I missed it and the tram carried on, I didn't know how far I would have to walk back. As it happened I was pleased that I had stuck to my original instructions, because as the bus approached the stop I could plainly see Miss Somers waiting for me on the corner. She had come in her own time to escort me up the dark tree-lined road, which she knew I was unfamiliar with. I was pleased to see her. We discussed the trams and buses but she decided it would still be better to use the bus as it was quicker.

On the way back to The Pines she told me that Mrs. Roberts had asked her to make enquiries at the boys home, 'Thornleigh', about my brother Clifford, and she had managed to telephone the housemother in charge who had told her that he was settling in well and attending the local school with the other boys. He was alright, she assured me.

"But what about my mother?" I asked, "Is <u>she</u> alright? Where is she?"

"Well I didn't get a chance to 'phone the place where your mother is" she said, but Miss Jackson, the person in charge at Thornleigh had told her that as my mother was not very well at present she was unable to get out to look for a new home for us, and for the moment she would be staying where she was.

"What's the matter with her?" I asked.

"Miss Jackson didn't know" she replied, adding that she would keep in touch with her and let me know any developments. In the meantime this conversation was just between the two of us as the only other person who knew about it was Mrs. Roberts.

As usual I cried myself to sleep that night, wondering how long it would be before my mother was better and able to look for a job.

* * *

Over the next few days and weeks, not only did I learn to navigate the route back to the home easily, quite often substituting the tram for the bus, but I also learned that I had time during my lunch break to get up to my <u>real</u> aunt's home, across the park and up the hill, to have a quick cup of tea occasionally. The first time I arrived it was quite a shock for her, as I entered by the back gate, which I knew was generally unlocked and knocked on her door. She was very surprised to see me but beckoned me inside, whereupon I had to explain how I came to be there.

As it turned out she already knew where my mother was but only that Clifford and I were now in a children's home. She did not know that we were separated, or where the homes were. I could only give her my own current address and also the name of Clifford's home, I didn't know where it was. I didn't have a great deal of time on that first visit as I had to get back to school, and after accepting tea and biscuits I dashed back. At least she now knew which school I was attending and promised to tell my brother Jack that she had seen me, when he came home from work later on.

Between them my brother and aunt managed to find out where we were all living and they were eventually contacted by my eldest brother Bill, who himself had received notification of all our whereabouts, being my mother's next of kin. On my subsequent lunchtime visits to my aunt I was told that my mother was 'bad with her nerves' and for the time being would remain where she was and Clifford and I should be thankful that we were being looked after properly and not wandering the streets! My mind was in turmoil. No mention had been made about visiting my sick mother and when I tried to press her further she said it was not up to her, it was for my brother Bill to make arrangements, he was now our legal guardian. Furthermore, she didn't think it was a good idea that I visited every day, two or three times a week would be enough. I silently thought that I was hoping that my mother would be better within a week or two and then I wouldn't be visiting my aunt at all!

However the weeks did accumulate and whilst I still had an acute heartache, longing to see my mother, I learned to cope with my situation. I was doing well at school and had at last been accepted by Mrs. Eaves, and I made friends, sometimes even 'skipping' school dinner and accompanying a friend to her home, where her mother gave us both what we liked. Her home was in the next street to my aunt and I was rather pleased with myself that I didn't feel the need to call in to see her on these occasions. I was still hurt that she didn't seem to be upset by our predicament.

One morning after I had been at The Pines for about six weeks, we girls were getting on with our usual cleaning of the dormitories when I had cause to get myself another polishing cloth. A bundle of old clothes was normally thrown by the staff into a corner of the landing for this purpose. As I approached I could see that today's bundle was made up of <u>my</u> clothes, the ones that I had arrived in and which as far as I knew lay in the store room, ready for when I went home. It was my best dress and jacket and still in good condition. I stood stock-still staring at the bundle, my heart pounding. A shout from Miss Norton told me to hurry up! Shaking and with a lump in my throat I picked up a pair of knickers also lying there and returned to the dormitory. As I worked the 'dummy' backwards and forwards I was sobbing.

By this time the staff was up to its normal complement of three, Mrs. Roberts was better and back at work and Miss Somers came in daily. The usual routine now was that Mrs. Roberts looked after the younger children, doing their hair and making breakfast and Miss Somers came in to help, starting with the cleaning. Miss Norton was still in charge. This enabled them to each have one day off duty per week, and a long weekend once every month. Two staff had to be available for duty each day. Miss Finch, who was a 'floater' came if the home was short-staffed. This strategy applied to all three children's homes, the girls', the boys', and the one that housed the under-fives.

On this particular day while I was still cleaning, Miss Somers arrived at work and as usual came upstairs to help, bringing with her a cup of tea for herself. As soon as she saw me she immediately recognised there was something upsetting me. Miss Norton had disappeared and so Miss Somers came up to me asking what was wrong. Between heart-rending sobs and pointing to the pile of clothes on the floor I managed to tell her. Her response was to give her cup of tea to me and telling me to drink it, she set off in pursuit of Miss Norton.

I had never seen Miss Somers angry before and was therefore surprised to hear her arguing with Miss Norton who had gone downstairs for some reason. By this time I had finished the tea and was back at work, and I could hear the two women shouting at each other as they made their way back to the landing. Miss Norton was insisting that she had meant no harm and they were summer clothes anyway, it was now winter and by next year I would have grown out of them. Miss Somers was not impressed, saying that a little thoughtfulness and kindness would not go amiss. She then took over my cleaning duties and told me to go downstairs for the usual wash and breakfast.

As I entered the kitchen Mrs. Roberts held out her open arms to me and I fell into them sobbing uncontrollably. As far as I was concerned this meant that I was not going to go home for a long time yet. Mrs. Roberts promised that she would try to find out more about my mother's health. The other children looked on in sympathy.

Chapter 13

TRIALS AND TRIBULATION

One day in late November I arrived back from school and entered the ablution room as usual. Everything was quiet and I wondered where everybody was. I followed my usual routine of hanging up my coat, washing my hands and climbing the flight of stone steps to the kitchen. I was amazed, when I entered, to find all the children sitting on the long church pew, each with their forefinger placed over their lips. Even the bigger girls were there and I noticed that Mary was grinning as she rocked herself to and fro, her finger slipping over her face. I asked if it was some kind of game at the same time as Miss Norton emerged from the scullery, scowling.

"No talking!" she stated, handing me a tea-cloth. "Dry those few cups in there and then get on with setting the table."

I did as I was bid and shortly afterwards she instructed everyone to take away their fingers and find their place at the table. This was done in silence.

This meant that we were all to have tea together, obviously a bit later than usual. My heart sank as all the children crowded around the table, the little ones standing to eat.

After giving the plates of food out and helping her to pour out the tea from the large tea-pot I had no option other than to take my place on a chair which another child had been made to vacate, to eat what she now placed in front of me. I hated this tea-time ritual of sharing the mugs of tea and usually managed to delay mine until the little ones had finished.

That evening Miss Norton was off duty and as Miss Somers was having a day off, Mrs. Roberts was in charge of bathing and eventually seeing us all into bed. I confided to her how much I disliked eating at the kitchen table and sharing the cups, and how I had witnessed the 'fingers on lips' routine. She did not reply in detail, only acknowledging that she was aware that it happened from time to time.

A few days later when I arrived home from school it was to find that everyone was in the dining room seated at tables of four, and that a place had been reserved for me. We were to use the dining room from now on and the places we now occupied were our permanent ones. Each girl had their own cup and saucer, also cutlery, and the serving table was in use. My seat was near to this table with my back to the majority of the other children. My three companions had reasonable table manners. The meal was served onto each plate by Miss Somers and given out to all by we older girls.

This mealtime change of venue meant that we girls would have to clear and re-set the tables after every meal and also it was another room that needed to be cleaned and polished every day. I didn't mind, it was wonderful news for me!

* * *

There was still no further news about my mother and brother and so I decided I would write my mother a letter. I chose to do this at school on a page carefully extracted from an exercise book. I told her where I was now living, that I was back at my old school, hoped she was feeling better and that I would like to have a letter from her. To make sure she knew she was loved and missed I carefully wrote out the words to two wartime songs, still popular at that time, altering a few words here and there to make them apply to my mother and not my sweetheart. The first two lines of one song ran: 'You are always in my heart, even though we're far apart.' The next song was 'We'll meet again'. I begged an envelope from my school friend's mother who, when she knew what I wanted it for, fixed me up with a stamp as well. I knew the address, having obtained it from my aunt some time previously. I posted the letter with some satisfaction. This one would not be confiscated by Miss Norton as my attempt to let my neighbour know how I was getting on had been, a few weeks ago. That night as I cried myself to sleep as usual I thought how pleased she would be to hear from me at last.

One lunchtime the following week I visited my aunt, who was displaying a long face when I arrived. She greeted me coolly and asked me what I had been doing writing a letter like that to my mother.

"What do you mean?" I asked.

"That letter written to your mother with the songs in it" she said crossly.

"How do you know about it?" I queried.

"Jack and I have been to see her" was her reply. "And she was very upset. You shouldn't have sent it."

I was stunned. Not only had they been to see my mother, without my knowledge, but it looked like they had seen the letter as well.

"Why can't I go to visit her as well?" I demanded.

"Because you're too young", she answered. "You've done untold damage with that letter".

"I only wanted her to know that I missed her" I defended myself.

"Well it's set her back" was all she would say.

As I left to go back to school I was both angry and upset.

Unknown to me at that time my mother was being kept in the institution against her will. The doctors had declared that she was unfit to be released when she had no home to return to and no-one to look after her. Both my brother Bill and my aunt had refused to take responsibility for her, each declaring their reasons.

My letter had only added to her deprivation, reinforcing the hopelessness of her situation. All she really needed at that time was a helping hand but when no-one would listen to her that she wanted to at least see her children, she rampaged through the corridors on a mission of vengeance. She was quickly subdued by trained staff but in effect had sealed her own fate. It was only a matter of time before my brother Bill would be approached, as next of kin, to consent to her admission to a mental hospital. Cited as evidence of her mental state was her refusal to work, her antagonism towards staff and an account of her walking naked through the corridors of the institution. In truth she had a severe nervous breakdown and in other circumstances could have been nursed back to health. Many years later I was told by a psychiatric nurse that one of the oldest 'tricks in the book' to get a patient certified mentally unfit, was to remove their clothes, giving them no other option than to walk about naked looking for the clothes. Fortunately I was married by then and able to handle this piece of information better than I would have at the time. My mother by then had already died.

Sometimes at weekends the children would have a visitor who would collect one or other of them and take them out for the day. Usually it was a relative of the child who turned up, but all visitors were previously selected by the child care officers, after application. The child would be told early that day in order to get ready, and always, without fail, it was a big event for the expectant girl. Some of these children were illiterate and had no idea of the time and consequently would be ready well in advance, sitting in the hall on yet another church pew wearing their outdoor clothes, waiting. Many times the visitor failed to arrive and the poor child would wait all morning not speaking, as the hall was normally out of bounds to the little ones and we bigger girls only passed by as we were doing our cleaning etc. Most of us had great sympathy with the forlorn child of course, who usually did not give up anticipating the arrival of their visitor, until they had to take off their coats and eat lunch. It always fell to Mrs. Roberts or Miss Somers to try to console them later on.

Mary had a regular visitor, her grown up sister, and she was always made welcome by Miss Norton who would greet her warmly by her Christian name and many times give her the use of her own room, so that she and Mary could spend some time together. This visitor always timed her visits to fit in with Miss Norton's week-ends on duty. Several years later I was to discover that Mary's sister was also her mother.

Another girl, Sally, who had natural curly hair, husky voice, and a winning smile was taken out every Saturday by a local woman. All the girls knew this woman as Auntie Brenda and most of them secretly wished she would take them out. She was young, small and vivacious and like a ray of sunshine when she came in to the home, laughing and making small talk. One day she did not come into the kitchen as usual but stayed talking in the hall with Miss Norton and Sally. Their voices were low and troubled, and the conversation went on for quite some time. At the end of it I was just in time to see a crying Sally sent up to bed as Miss Norton returned to the kitchen after closing the front door behind Auntie Brenda. Sally was to be punished even further the following week when her sister was taken out in her place, but eventually after a cooling-off period the visits and outings went on as before. I never did find out what misdemeanour she had committed.

Both these girls, Sally and her sister, slept in my dormitory, and bade each other a special 'good-night' every night. Maureen the elder of the two was the girl nearest to the light-switch, by the door, and Sally slept in a corner bed. One morning, just after getting up I heard a piercing scream coming from Maureen's direction and was aghast to see her jumping up and down on the bed whilst emitting her screams. Mrs. Roberts entered the room, which in itself was unusual, her duties at morning were normally downstairs, and tried to get hold of her. Maureen was having none of it and continued to jump up and down, arms and legs hitting out. I couldn't believe my eyes as I witnessed the performance until I heard her demand:-

"Where is she? What have you done with her?"

I looked towards Sally's bed and realised instantly that not only was it empty but it had been re-made. Even so I didn't think it was worth all the shouting.

Maureen however knew differently, whether by instinct or maybe being forewarned that it might happen, I never found out, but Sally had gone and Maureen was devastated. We were all surprised; we had all witnessed their 'good-night' kiss the previous evening. Mrs. Roberts did her best to console her but her bereft cries went on for days. It wasn't Auntie Brenda who had taken Sally; she had been taken and adopted by a new family, no-one knew where. Sally was eight years old; Maureen was ten. We never saw Auntie Brenda again either.

* * *

One evening, a few weeks before Christmas, a new girl came to live at the home. When I first saw her I was delighted. She looked about my age and was smiling, which showed up a dimple in her cheek. She was nearly as tall as me but heavier built. Her name was Hazel. Miss Somers was on duty, alone, and told me to take Hazel downstairs to the ablution room to show her where to hang her coat, and wash her hands and face. Once downstairs I selected a peg for her and then she turned and ran towards the cellar steps, bounding up them before I had had time to say a few words of welcome. I tried to talk to her from behind, on the steps, but she shunned me with a distinct action of annoyance.

Once inside the kitchen she prowled around like a tiger, and Miss Somers asked me how I had gone on downstairs.

"I couldn't get her to talk to me" I said, "She seemed annoyed with me."

"Never mind" Miss Somers replied, "She's not very communicative. It's not your fault."

It turned out that Hazel was mentally disturbed, obviously disruptive, and unable to go to school, more often than not acting like a bull in a china shop. In time her happy nature would be discovered but this only came to the surface when she got her own way. My hopes of having someone of my own age to talk to were dashed.

However, Hazel became a firm favourite with the staff although they always had to be aware of her turn of moods and of her strength. Not being at school meant that she could help with the cleaning and she would get hold of the 'dummy' to work the polish into the floor, with a vengeance, muttering to herself all the time she was active. If Miss Finch happened to be around she would joke with her telling her she was not as good as <u>she</u> was and Hazel would work her socks off, standing breathless at the side of the room afterwards, while Miss Finch did the final polish. At mid-morning break she would be rewarded with a chocolate biscuit and milk. She had a stammer and on being asked what she had earned by doing good work she would say: "ch.ch.ch. Chocolate," with a sideways movement of her arm against her body in time with the stammer. She had a beautiful smile and knew when she was amusing the staff.

* * *

I still missed my mother and brother dreadfully and, as December arrived, having had no news of them for a few weeks, I began to realise that I wasn't going to be out in time for Christmas. I was not looking forward to Christmas at all. I had grown accustomed to schooldays and at least the travelling and lessons got the days over for me, but I wondered what the winter school holiday would be like. I frequently asked Mrs. Roberts and Miss Somers if they had any news for me, but both said they had no news of my mother and Clifford was doing very well at school.

"What use is that to me?" I silently wondered, angrily.

I expected Clifford to do well at school, but was he happy? I realised that most of the time I was sad and <u>unhappy</u> and knew that he would be too. I wondered if I could get some money to get presents for them. I resolved to ask Mrs. Roberts if she could help me.

Chapter 14

CHRISTMAS

As Christmas approached more children were admitted to the home, sometimes a single child, sometime two sisters, and by the time mid-December arrived The Pines had a 'full house' - all beds occupied. It was decided therefore by Miss Norton that as the oldest girl, I would have to sleep in the attic room and a bed was prepared for me on top of the pile of spare mattresses. I didn't mind this as I liked nothing better than to be on my own, but Mrs. Roberts objected to the way the bed was formed, and eventually an iron bedstead was found for me with only two or three mattresses piled on, the others being stored upright against the wall. I was using only a small corner of the huge attic room, and screens were placed alongside the bed in an attempt to make it less draughty. I slept soundly, did not fall off, as anticipated, and was woken in the usual manner every morning.

I loved the independence of being on my own and many times would go over to the tiny window and look out at the dark night, listening to the owl which lived in the trees. Being on my own also meant that I could have a light on to read the magazines passed on to me by Mrs. Roberts.

Most of the long-term children, especially the older ones, knew the procedure for Christmas. We would have a big tree in the hall, I was told, a special meal on Christmas Day, and the attic playroom where I now slept would be used to play with the toys given out to all the children.

Miss Norton decorated the hall, it took her over two weeks to do this, and I was aware that both Miss Somers and Mrs. Roberts refused to help. The end result was very pretty but not in keeping at all with Christmas. It was a succession of overhead arches made by bending cane to stretch from wall to wall, the width of the hall. These were then decorated with pink paper flowers resembling apple-blossom, painstakingly made by Miss Norton. This must have been a theme she either dreamt up or had witnessed somewhere else. It was a spring theme really and the Christmas tree in the corner seemed out of place! When she asked me if I liked it I didn't answer at first, but she carried on to say it was pretty, so I had to agree. Meanwhile Mrs. Roberts, Miss Somers and I made paper chains to hang in the dining room. Whilst we were making the paper chains I talked with them about past Christmases and told them of the good ones I remembered when I was little. I tried unsuccessfully to broach the subject of presents for my family; they both told me that Clifford would have a good Christmas at the boys home, just as we would at The Pines, and whenever I talked about my mother there was no feed back. I tried to make the best of my situation and was grateful to have 'adult' conversation sometimes.

* * *

End of school term eventually arrived and I was therefore now a virtual prisoner in the home, my independent travel to and from school where I could 'shake-off' my label of being different, curtailed for the time being. I was assigned many tasks within the home to fill these last few days before Christmas, all of which I did thoroughly as was my nature, but none of which I truthfully enjoyed. Once school had finished the little ones knew that Christmas was not far away and began to get excited but all I could still think about was going 'home', or at least being allowed to see my mother. Not going to school at this time meant that I had absolutely no way of even finding out how she was. I was completely unaware that she had already been transferred to a mental hospital near Preston.

* * *

Christmas day eventually arrived and as predicted by the other children everyone had a present at the end of their bed, which we were allowed to open before breakfast. Bed making and cleaning were cut to a minimum, but polishing the centre of the room with the 'dummy' still undertaken by we older girls before getting washed and dressed, followed by breakfast in the dining room. The young ones were then allowed up in the attic playroom under supervision whilst we older ones cleaned up the breakfast dishes and re-set the dining room for lunch.

All in all the staff did their best to make the day special for the children, the lunch was good and some time during the day Father Christmas appeared in the attic, complete with sack full of toys which he distributed according to age, with help from the staff. I suppose I was given a few gifts but the only one I can remember was a lovely little sequined evening purse, which I still have today. It represented 'frivolity and glamour' to me, sadly lacking in my life at the time. The next day I remember swapping another of my presents with a girl who had been given a game of 'Draughts' but she did not know how to play it. Again I still have the game.

One of the children had been given a kaleidoscope - a tube which if shaken would produce different patterns made by small pieces of coloured glass, reflected in a mirror at the bottom of the tube, which could be viewed by holding the kaleidoscope to the eye. The patterns were extremely pretty and colourful, adding a touch of 'magic' to an otherwise drab life. After just one look down the tube Hazel claimed it for herself! She adored it and spent hours looking and smiling, occasionally lowering it to try to stammer out the beauty she beheld, but she had an iron grip and was of strong build and no other child would dare to try to take it from her. As she did not have the capability of playing with other toys this kaleidoscope was like manna from heaven to her and it rarely left her side. The staff even let her take it into the dining room with her and all the children accepted this.

The attic playroom continued to be used for several more days after Christmas but apart from sleeping there I rarely went of my own free will. If left unsupervised the children ran riot, making an incredible din, and unless I was detailed to supervise, I kept away, much preferring to wash up etc

Eventually things got back to normal, the Christmas tree was dismantled and the decorations put away, with the exception of the pink flower display in the hall. This was still up as the following Easter approached.

Before that of course it was back to school, much to my delight. I wondered how far into 1948 we would get before my family could be re-united.

Chapter 15

ACCEPTING MY LOT

Once I was back at school I very quickly slipped into the routine I had developed the previous term, of walking down the road on which the home was situated in order to catch the bus or tram which would take me to school. Once there – still in Mrs. Eaves' class I got stuck into my lessons, worked hard and looked forward to my lunch time excursions with my friend Marina, either hanging around the local shop with the other schoolchildren, or quite often I would accompany her home, where her mother once more gave us special tit-bits. All of this meant normality to me and I hungered for it.

Sometimes on these excursions I stopped off at my aunt's house to have a cup of tea with her. On these occasions Marina would go to her home nearby and when it was time to return to school we would meet up and joyfully run through the park to get back in time. Whilst at my aunt's of course I would always ask about my mother, and so it was that towards the end of January she told me that my mother was in hospital at Preston and as visiting was allowed once every month she would be going to see her sister the following Saturday; my brother Jack would be going with her. She then proceeded to quote from a mental list the things my mother had asked her to bring when she visited – tea, powdered milk, writing paper and stamps, a comb, and a few other bits she needed.

"How do you know she needs these things?" I queried. Will she be coming out soon?"

Of course it was then that I discovered that my mother had written to my aunt, who in any case already knew where her sister was, as my brother Bill, being next of kin, had been notified of her admission to the hospital. I was dumbfounded that everyone else in the family, except Clifford and I, had known for several weeks where my mother now was, and had decided not to tell me. I accepted that they couldn't tell Clifford because they were not in touch with him but I was angry, to say the least, that they had sent her a Christmas card and I had not been allowed to. I demanded from my aunt my mother's address. If I couldn't go to visit her I was determined to write.

She was loathe to give it to me, saying that she would probably already be in trouble with the authorities for informing me that mother was in hospital and after the last episode of my trying to comfort her with a letter, another communication could only mean trouble! I wondered why.

Eventually, after much cajoling, and after promising that I wouldn't write any more songs, she gave me my mother's latest letter, to read. I then realised, from the heading at the top of the letter, that she was in a mental hospital. However the contents of the letter were normal enough and it brought a lump to my throat as I saw my beloved mother's handwriting once more. Apart from the requests for the few items already mentioned, her main request was that my aunt brought with her Clifford and I, if at all possible.

Of course I pounced on this request, begging her to take me with her and as I started to cry and shout my disappointment, she threw her arms up in the air saying <u>that</u> was the reason I hadn't been told, because it would obviously upset me! I quietened down, I knew that I wasn't going to get any further information if I didn't behave responsibly

My aunt promised to tell my mother all about me and that I sent my love and that she couldn't take me with her because only two visitors were allowed, and Jack was to accompany her. I couldn't argue with any of this but said that I <u>was</u> going to write a letter, which unfortunately would have to be posted as it was now too late for me to write it and then give it to my aunt by visiting day, Saturday. She suggested that I called on her again on Monday of the following week and she would then tell me all about her visit, and if I had written my letter by then, she would post it for me. I silently vowed that I would post it myself once I had managed to get a stamp from somewhere. I memorised the address.

Before leaving to go back to school I asked <u>why</u> my mother was in a mental hospital. I was told that she had 'bad nerves' for which she would receive treatment in that kind of hospital. Until she was better there was no possibility of her setting up home on her own. I didn't wait for Marina that day, I walked back to school shedding intermittent tears. When Marina caught up with me we walked the rest of the way in silence, although she did not know of my troubled thoughts.

* * *

I could hardly wait for the following Monday to arrive; at last I would be able to hear first-hand knowledge of my mother. I had not kept it secret from Mrs. Roberts that I occasionally visited my aunt in my lunch break from school and therefore over the week-end I told her of my aunt's admission to me where my mother now was, and that she intended to visit her. She said that my mother was now in the best place to get better, but that it would probably take several weeks, and to be aware when I received my aunt's report that patients had good days and bad days. She advised me not to write my letter until after I had seen my aunt.

However when I arrived breathless at my aunt's house on Monday lunchtime I was not prepared for the detailed information she gave me. On entering the hospital they had been asked detailed questions about their relationship to the patient and also, further information regarding the patient's background sought. My aunt and brother notified them about Clifford and me and were told that we would not be allowed to visit until we were fourteen years of age. I was not yet thirteen! However I fervently believed that mother would get better before then.

Once they had passed through security in reception they were allowed to see my mother but only under supervision, and when they broke the news that we were not able to visit until we were older, she once again went to pieces, demanding to be let out, begging my aunt to take her home with her. The staff eventually calmed her down, threatening not to allow any visitors at all if she didn't behave; my mother complied and only when it was time for her visitors to leave did she shed any more tears. She told my aunt to tell me that she would answer my letter when I wrote.

It was another month before the next visit was allowed and this time my aunt went with my brother Bill. Meanwhile, Mrs. Roberts had fixed me up with writing materials and I had written my letter, given it to Mrs. Roberts to post, but had not received a reply. After this second visit my aunt informed me that mother was not well and receiving treatment, and it would be for the best if I didn't write any more letters for the time being.

* * *

During these first few months of 1948 I didn't see my brother Clifford, or either of my other two brothers, but I worried constantly about Clifford and my mother. Adults all around me seemed to think that all was going reasonably well but I found it difficult to accept the situation, privately thinking that I <u>knew</u> how they would both be feeling whereas the rest of my family and my new found friends Mrs. Roberts and Miss Somers did not care about them in the same way that I did. I felt that at different times, my aunt and both my brothers, had let my mother down, and Mrs. Roberts and Miss Somers although kind, did not really know them. I still hated the world!

I threw my energies into my schoolwork, as strangely enough learning was my only pleasure these days, and slowly I worked my way towards being in the top ten pupils in my class.

I still visited my aunt and Marina's mother occasionally during my lunch break but quite often I just passed the time hanging around with other pupils gossiping. I was learning to accept my lot, but I never lost hope that we would all be together again someday. As far as the other pupils knew I was still living with my aunt until my mother got better. I never informed them differently.

However there was one other person to whom I was obliged to tell my address and that was the school secretary. She was a nice lady who usually caught the same bus as I did on our way to school every morning. She began by smiling at me as we waited at the bus stop, then gradually I became aware that she was the school secretary and I said "hello" each day, and then one morning once we were on the bus, sitting side by side, she confided that she had seen me several times in church. I was mortified and felt my face flush crimson as I realised that she <u>knew</u> I was in the children's home, with my short hair tied with a ribbon, and of course she had seen me with the other children. I of course had not noticed her. I then acknowledged that I did go to the local church with the other children. During the conversation I explained that I did not go to the local school however as I had been allowed to continue at my old school, where she was secretary, as I would be going home again soon, living in that area. I also told her that my school friends did not know that I was in a children's home, and she gently squeezed my hand and told me not to worry – she would not tell them, but it was after all, nothing to be ashamed of.

Chapter 16

1948

For the first few months of 1948 nothing in my life changed very much. I followed the same routine as already described, the daily monotonous tasks of bed making, cleaning etc., going to and from school, and church on Sundays. Most Saturdays the children were sent out to tidy the garden if the weather was dry and extra jobs inside undertaken if it was wet. I had no news of my mother and although I continually asked Mrs. Roberts and Miss Somers for news of Clifford I was always met with the same reply, that he was fine and doing well at school. I still cried myself to sleep most nights, knowing that he wouldn't be aware that I knew how he was faring and so I worried that he was even more miserable than I was. By this time I was back in my dormitory bed as the number of children needing accommodation had been reduced.

As spring approached and the days got longer several things seemed to happen at the same time. It was arranged with the local cinema that most of the children in the home could go along, accompanied by an adult, and sit in the better seats at the rear of the cinema every Saturday afternoon, to watch the matinee. Of course we had to walk there in the usual 'crocodile' formation. The Saturday afternoon treat did at least help break the monotony. However after the first couple of times, the staff decided that they didn't look forward to this outing and so it was arranged that I would take only the well-behaved girls on my own. This still numbered approximately sixteen of us and it was quite a task for me to keep order. To make matters worse we were quite conspicuous both in the manner of our arrival and also because we had to sit on our own, segregated from the rest of the audience. The cinema staff stood at the back throughout the performance, and always made sure we were off the premises before releasing the rest!

Possibly because she felt sorry for me, or maybe because she was a kind person anyway, Miss Somers, who was a Salvationist, began to take me along with her to the Sunday evening meetings at her local citadel, whenever it was convenient. Sometimes of course it was not her evening off and so we didn't go anywhere. I enjoyed these excursions, going by bus together after she had finished work for the day, and in truth I also enjoyed the meetings, the singing and the friendliness of the congregation. Afterwards Miss Somers would accompany me to my final bus stop, where she would see me safely on the bus, making sure that the conductor knew where I was to get off at the end of my journey. I would then walk down the tree-lined road to the home, as the nights were lighter now.

About this time, probably around Easter, Mrs. Roberts decided to take me home with her on her day off. This was only possible during school holidays of course, and was a measure of this lovely lady's good nature that she was virtually giving up her day of rest to make my life a little brighter. I wasn't much trouble of course, being quite a grown-up thirteen year old (almost.) We had to travel by bus to her home town of Bolton, in the evening, after she had finished work for the day, and then after staying at her family home with her own mother overnight, we spent a pleasant day, shopping in the town centre, meeting up with friends and relatives and generally relaxing before making the return journey. Mrs. Roberts had been widowed in her early married life after just eight months of marriage, and had no children of her own.

* * *

School life in this period went on as normal, my occasional visits to my aunt not bringing forth any more news about my mother. Visits to the hospital were still not allowed, not even for the adults, for the time being, and neither Miss Somers nor Mrs. Roberts could get Miss Jackson at the boys home to allow me to see Clifford.

A short time after returning to school after Easter, I was informed by Mrs. Eaves that a few pupils in her class were to be allowed to take another examination by the education authority, to gain entrance to technical or commercial colleges for children aged thirteen. I would be thirteen in early May and would therefore qualify. It was a last-chance effort for the few pupils she had recommended, to further their education. I had better get down to studying even harder than at present! She added that the final outcome would make a big difference to my life. And so it was that in late May or early June I arrived at Stockport town hall to once again try my luck with a scholarship.

Unfortunately for me when I sat this examination I was to discover that more than 50% of the questions were based on general knowledge and current affairs. The English and arithmetic papers were no trouble to me, but how could I be expected to know the name of the prime minister when newspapers and radio were not available at the home and we were not taught current affairs at school? On completion, I was aware that I had not done well.

* * *

Eventually after about six weeks the dozen or so of we pupils who had taken the examination were called in as a group to the headmaster's office. He was a very abrupt man, I think nearing the end of his career, and always appeared to be angry and bad tempered about something!

After arranging us in a semi-circle in front of his desk he began to read aloud the names of the pupils who had passed the entrance examination, looking up as each name was read to ascertain which pupil it referred to; I am quite sure that he did not actually recognise any of us. When he had finished, approximately half of those present were in the happy position of knowing that a new and better school awaited them. I was not one of them.

Eventually he threw his pen down on the desk, sat back in his chair and scowled at the group as a whole, indicating that none of us were of great credit to the school as even the ones who had passed were lucky to have had a second chance, and as for the rest of us - words failed him!

"You!" he eventually bellowed to a boy on my right. "What will your father have to say when you tell him the result?" The boy mumbled that he didn't know.

"And you!" he said, pointing at me. "What will <u>your</u> father have to say? What's your name again?"

Trembling, I told him my name and that my father had died.

Not hesitating for a second, he angrily shouted "Well what about your mother then, what will <u>she</u> think? Did she <u>think</u> you were going to pass?"

"My mother's in hospital" I replied, darting an anxious look at my friend Mrs. Wilson, the school secretary, who was hovering in the background.

"Whom do you live with then?" he almost screamed at me.

"A lady" I faltered, my pleading eyes looking at Mrs. Wilson.

By this time, to my relief, she had moved over to her boss and was whispering in his ear.

My relief was short-lived however as he screamed at me "Why didn't you tell me in the first place that you were in a home?"

There were gasps of astonishment from my fellow pupils as Mrs. Wilson leant on a filing cabinet with her head in her hands and I burst into tears.

I am sure that he wasn't aware of the surprise and consternation he had created as he angrily told us all to clear off!

Word quickly spread in school that I was in a home and of course nearly everyone thought it was one for naughty children, as that was the only kind we knew about. I spent several days thereafter fending off questions and at the same time trying to let everyone know that it was just temporary, whilst my mother was in hospital. My friend Marina supported me as she and her mother had known all along, but she had kept my secret.

Shortly after this episode the headmaster again went off work sick, and as far as I am aware never returned to school. He certainly was not in his office when school resumed again for the autumn term, after the long summer break.

Chapter 17

SCHOOL HOLIDAYS

When school finished for the summer holiday break I knew that I would once again have to face spending long days cooped up in the home, with only the occasional odd treat from one of the staff, whenever they could fit it in. There was one difference however, as by now the summer evenings stretched until at least nine-o-clock. It was decided that on Saturdays instead of going to the cinema, provided I could make suitable arrangements with my aunt, I could visit her and stay for tea, returning in the early evening. Of course I resumed contact with her and the visits began. I walked to and from her house, dressed in smart clothes which I was allowed to wear just for these visits. The clothes had actually been sent from America as gifts to three sisters in the home, by a relative, but although all three girls were much younger than I, they were all stoutly built and so unable to wear them. I didn't give much thought to the girls as I set off on my excursions, after all I had been told to wear the clothes by the staff, but looking back I can see that they were probably upset, as they knew they belonged to them and as far as I am aware they hadn't even been consulted!

Whilst making these visits to my aunt I sometimes called in to see my friend Marina and occasionally, by deviating from my normal route, I would visit my brother Bill and his wife and baby in their rented rooms, always endeavouring to find out any information I could about my mother and younger brother.

About this time visits to my mother were once again resumed, on the last Saturday of every month, my brother Jack and aunt visiting alternately with brother Bill. Although I pleaded constantly with Bill to take me with him, he never would. He always went alone. Jack however promised to 'test the water' on his visits and see if it was possible to 'sneak me in'. I waited patiently for several months.

* * *

August being a full month of school holidays, it was decided by the local council that all children in care should be sent on a camping holiday for two weeks. It was not just Stockport council that did this, other surrounding district councils were also involved in the scheme; staff from each care home were designated to accompany the children. Miss Somers and Miss Finch were to be our particular guardians, and joy of joys for me, I learned that as the boys from Thornleigh would also be going at the same time, I would at last be able to see Clifford; the first time for nearly twelve months.

We set off on a hired bus for our destination in north Wales, arriving mid-afternoon on a wet Saturday. By tea-time several other buses had delivered their cargo of children and there were approximately two hundred of us. As each bus arrived the occupants were lined up at different tables and given a different coloured ribbon to wear across the shoulder for identification. Boys and girls were segregated.

We had arrived at a huge playing field, situated just off the main road between Rhyl and Abergele in north Wales. What I can only presume were ex-army circular tents, were placed in regimental fashion awaiting us for sleeping arrangements.

Eventually we were taken by our carers to a large wooden building which was the dining room. Here we all dined together, but it was too big for me to find Clifford easily.

After tea we were all directed to ablution huts and then given a number to identify our tents for sleeping, each tent holding eight girls with a senior girl to keep order. Our senior was aged about sixteen or seventeen and was probably a girl guide. She quickly showed us how to undress whilst kneeling on our sleeping bags, all of which were arranged with our feet at a central pole, the only place where the tent was high enough for us to stand up. She stood there and gave orders. When we eventually got into our sleeping bags she placed hers across the tent exit; I naively wondered why. She had previously told us that if anyone needed the toilet during the night, we had to wake her. It was still raining the next morning and as it turned out it rained more or less continuously for the full fortnight.

After ablutions and breakfast we were all assigned tasks such as peeling potatoes, cleaning toilets etc. and helping in the kitchen, according to age. I seemed to be allocated tasks with other youngsters of approximately the same age but none of whom I knew. Whilst going about these tasks I occasionally saw Miss Somers or Miss Finch shepherding the younger children from The Pines into various tents and huts, and when possible they asked me how I was getting on. They themselves had been allocated wooden huts to sleep in, along with some of the younger children.

We all trooped into the dining hut again for mid-day meal and sat at our numbered table to eat and swap stories. All our younger girls had spent the morning in a tent singing songs etc. We older girls had finished our jobs and the afternoon was to be spent in recreation. It was still raining hard. I had still not seen Clifford.

It was to be another two or three days before I came face to face with him, and then only because Miss Somers had gone in search of him for me as I could not do this for myself because of the segregation. He was easily recognisable to me as he approached the spot where Miss Somers had told me to wait, but how he had changed! He was taller of course and his face had filled out and become more mature; he had a far more confident attitude than the young boy I had last seen the previous year.

He was pleased to see me but not enthused, and we did not embrace. He was slightly out of breath, having followed Miss Somers across the campsite at a run. She had explained to him that I had been looking for him for a couple of days and just wanted to say 'hello'. However after we both asked each other if everything was alright, he was eager to return to the game of football he had just left as even though the ground we stood upon was a sea of mud, at least it had stopped raining for a while. There was nothing further to say and so with a smile and a wave he ran back the way he had come. I briefly saw him a couple of times after that from a distance. Of course he too had had to adjust to his circumstances and accept his lot. Miss Jackson was right, he <u>had</u> settled down and he was mixing with boys of his own age. In the days that followed I found that this meeting had left me curiously content as I acknowledged that he could now take care of himself!

Somehow we all got through that dreadful 'holiday', sliding about in the mud. Occasionally we older girls were allowed into nearby Abergele, always taken in the regulation 'crocodile' and always under supervision. There wasn't much to do even in the town but at least we escaped the wet canvas flapping against us!

At last it was time to leave and this time I was able to seek Clifford out for myself, as we all got ready to board the buses. He took this opportunity to ask me if I had any news of our mother and Jack, and as far as I remember I told him mother was in a hospital, with bad nerves, and in exchange he told me that Jack had written to him. He confirmed that he was alright, but I was left feeling that he was putting on a good front.

When we girls finally arrived back at The Pines, Mrs. Roberts awaited us and I could hardly believe that I was actually glad to be back! I stood with Miss Somers whilst she related to Mrs. Roberts all we had endured.

"Mavis was counting the days to come home. Weren't you?" she added, turning to me. I nodded in agreement, amazed that she had understood me so well.

Chapter 18

MOVING ON

As the long summer school holiday drew to a close I knew I would shortly be going back to school and into a new class. This was known as the top class and in fact covered two years tuition in the one class, the new intake replacing the previous year's class and the established ones replacing the pupils who had now left school. There were actually two top classes, one for the girls and one for the boys. The boys were taught by a disciplinarian, the girls were not. I was not looking forward to returning to school. However the new term finally began and the first day was spent getting acquainted with our new surroundings.

By mid-day it was apparent to me that although we, the new intake, were happy to buckle down to lessons, there was a section of older girls who were not going to let it happen. There was no respect for the teacher whatsoever and the majority of the girls in this class sat around applying make-up etc. and generally making a nuisance of themselves. They were also on the look-out for new recruits. We were not willing candidates, as in our previous class, taught by Mrs. Eaves, we had had to be well behaved.

Our new teacher had a cane, which hardly ever left her side, and during the afternoon as she was attempting to maintain order by moving about between desks with girls either sitting on top of them or standing around chatting, she was swishing it around the girls. Suddenly as she tried to make the ring-leader sit down, the girl, who was quite well built and had an aggressive attitude, snatched it from her and started to chase her around the room, using the cane as a weapon. She was shouting and swearing as she did so. She did not let up and so the teacher had to protect herself as best she could until the girl finally drove her outside into the corridor. From her position inside the classroom she then taunted the teacher, ridiculing her.

I was horrified as we all witnessed this exhibition and I tried to keep away from the crowd now surrounding the culprit. Teacher was still in the corridor but as soon as she moved away, ostensibly to get the headmaster, the girl picked up her belongings and left the classroom. By the time teacher returned, accompanied by another senior teacher, as the headmaster was not in school, the class had settled down somewhat. I had not liked what I had witnessed and groaned inwardly at what was to come. If this was a sample of what life in this class was like, I was going to hate it just as much as I hated staying at The Pines.

* * *

At some point during the following day the whole class was sent out to the nearby park playing field for a games lesson. The game was hockey; it was the start of the season and therefore the first game I had ever taken part in or even witnessed. As our class teacher had not returned to school that day, we were being supervised by the school P.E. teacher.

Once she had established the rules of the game, pointing out that the captain would start by 'bullying off', attempting to get the first shot at the ball with the hockey stick once the signal had been given to start, she asked for two volunteers to be captains of opposing teams. Yesterday's ring-leader immediately put herself forward, grabbing a hockey stick and swinging it to get the 'feel of it'. No one else volunteered.

"Right. You" she said, thrusting a stick into the hands of the nearest girl, who just happened to be me. "You are the opposing captain. Get ready to bully off".

I duly moved to the central spot she had indicated, with my team behind me, stood with feet apart and body bent over the ball as instructed and chanted the words previously demonstrated by her, "One-a-bully, two-a-bully, three-a-bully - OFF" at the same time clicking hockey sticks with my opponent, prior to hitting the ball, hopefully before she did.

Of course this was well nigh impossible for me, I didn't stand a chance against her aggressive manner. Up came the hard hockey ball before the word "three" was even uttered. It was delivered with such force straight into my face that it knocked me off balance and I crumpled, throwing away the stick and clutching my left eye. Blood was pouring down my face and onto my clothes as willing hands lifted me to a standing position. The girl in question was stood somewhat apart from my little group, laughing and gesticulating, indicating that she was ready to have another go.

The damage to my face and eye could not be estimated out on the playing field as it needed cleaning up, and as the P.E. teacher (who barely knew any of us) had no back-up, she was forced to abandon the game as she escorted me back to school. I was clutching some sort of cloth to my eye and crying as we made our way back, followed by the rest of the class. The headmaster was still not in school and so two other teachers were recruited to give an opinion on the condition of my eye. I could tell they were worried about any lasting damage. Eventually, after many questions, it was decided that the blood was coming from a rather deep cut high on my cheekbone, just under the eye socket, and it appeared that the eye itself was not damaged.

I was naturally feeling shocked and sick, with a headache, at the end of the afternoon, and it was therefore decided that one of the teachers, the only one who owned a car, would take me home. In the event he took me only as far as the bottom of the long driveway leading up to the home, and I made my weary way up towards the entrance, only being able to see out of one eye. A bandage covered the other, held down by sticking plaster.

I entered by the boot-room door as usual, and as I slowly climbed the cellar steps to the kitchen my head was pounding. I could hear the noise made by the young children talking and shouting as they waited for Miss Norton to give them their tea-time meal, even before I entered. I was earlier than usual, having been brought back by car and everyone was surprised to see me, especially in the condition I was in. Even Miss Norton showed concern, and of course I had to relate all that had happened to me.

By evening, when Mrs. Roberts came on duty, I was feeling rather worse for wear; my head was still pounding, my face ached, I had not felt like eating, and I was desperate to lie down. Mrs. Roberts had been informed of my condition by Miss Norton, and the first thing she did was to give me some of her own aspirin tablets. She then told me to go to her room and lie on her bed for a while. I gladly complied. Once the younger children were in bed she brought me some hot milk and I told her my sorry tale. I was glad to get into my own bed that night.

I did not go to school the following day, my head and face still ached and my left eye was closed. After cleansing it, Mrs. Roberts put a new dressing on and an eye patch was found for me. This tightened the dressing underneath and I felt more comfortable. The cut on my cheekbone was still very open and prone to bleeding and I was aware that 'stitching' was being discussed. I was told that Matron would be inspecting it later when she came for lunch.

In the end after much questioning it was decided that any stitching required should have been done the previous day and it was better to leave it to heal naturally now. My face was still swollen and the eye closed, but I could be sent to school the next day.

I had a miserable time for the next two days. Our teacher had returned but was obviously unable to teach the trouble-maker, who never showed any contrition towards me but rather revelled in the pandemonium she was causing. There being no head-teacher to expel her she was removed from the girls class and put in with the boys. I was glad when the week drew to a close and I made my weary way back to The Pines.

I climbed the cellar steps late that afternoon feeling very sorry for myself, with nothing to look forward to, it was even difficult to read the magazines Mrs. Roberts sometimes passed on to me, with only one good eye. My only consolation was that it was Miss Norton's weekend off and Mrs. Roberts would be back from <u>her</u> day off that night. As I entered the kitchen Miss Somers was preparing tea.

On seeing me, and asking how I was feeling, she quickly shepherded the rest of the children into the dining room and in an abrupt manner told me to join them. This was unusual as I normally helped, carrying the food into the dining room etc.

"Everybody, except Mavis Bailey, sit down" she said, as she moved to the centre of the room, indicating that I should stand next to her.

Her voice was very serious as she addressed the other children, all seated by now, looking expectantly towards the two of us.

"Does anybody <u>know</u> what Mavis Bailey has done?" she enquired looking around as if she expected an answer.

"She's moved her bandage," someone said.

I was at a loss to even contemplate how I could have upset Miss Somers and my heart sank as I anticipated even more misery to come.

"No, it's nothing to do with her bandage" she declared, "It's much more important than that!" After a slight pause: "She's only passed her scholarship, that's all!"

I was startled, and looked up from my downcast expression to see her smiling at me with arms open to give me a quick hug.

"She will be going to a new school," she concluded.

My uppermost thought was that I would not have to go back to my old one, and I checked this out with her. She smiled as she confirmed that I would not, and I realised that she understood how much I hated it.

That evening when the children had been put to bed, I was allowed to rest in the staff sitting room, so that I would still be up and able to give Mrs. Roberts the good news when she returned. The three of us quietly celebrated with a cup of tea.

Of course Mrs. Roberts wanted to know why it had taken so long to inform me that I had passed the exam, taken three months earlier, and it was left to Miss Somers to fill us in as best she could.

Apparently Matron had arrived that lunch-time with the news, having been contacted by the education department of our town council. She had brought with her a copy of a letter which had been sent in late June addressed to Mrs. Bailey, informing her that her daughter was to be offered a place at Stockport Junior Commercial School, to commence early September. The letter had been addressed to Mrs. Bailey at The Pines, followed by the correct address. Somehow the letter had gone astray. Matron had now arranged for me to start at the school, part of Stockport College for further education, early the following week.

The two women looked at each other with knowing looks. Neither of them was aware of a letter arriving addressed to my mother, but they would make enquiries.

In the meantime congratulations were in order, it was just a shame that I had gone back to my old school and finished up with a black eye!

Chapter 19

COMMERCIAL SCHOOL

The following Monday morning Mrs. Roberts accompanied me to Stockport College, where we hoped to find the Junior Commercial School and she could explain to the head of the school why I had not commenced at the beginning of term. Finding the correct part of the college proved quite difficult however and I was glad that Mrs. Roberts was with me. It was towards mid-morning when we eventually made our way to a completely different building situated in a back street, running parallel with the main highway. This building turned out to be a Wesleyan Sunday school, rented by Stockport town council and utilised as a day school. It had two storeys, a fine staircase, and an assembly hall, equipped with a stage.

I felt very conspicuous as we climbed the staircase in search of someone in authority.

I had spent the weekend, assisted by Mrs. Roberts and Miss Somers, making my clothes look presentable, but of course

I had never received the official 'follow up' letter informing the students where the school building was situated and what kind of uniform we would be expected to wear. In addition, the few students I had seen so far all seemed to be much more grown up than I, and certainly didn't have short straight hair! They didn't sport black eyes either, and I felt that we incurred many curious looks as we went up and down the staircase.

At last someone directed us to the headmaster's office, situated immediately at the bottom of the staircase, and we were eventually admitted. Actually Mrs. Roberts had a private word with the headmaster prior to my admittance and I think between them they discovered why I had not been told at my old school that I had gained the scholarship. My previous headmaster was working from a list of pupils who were to be offered a place at designated colleges after the initial examination. Should any of those pupils not accept the place offered, it would then be offered to a student further down the list, according to the ability indicated by the marks gained. In other words, I had just scraped in, after someone had refused a place at Stockport Junior Commercial School! A letter to this effect would have been sent to the parents or guardians of the child concerned, at a later date.

After giving Mrs. Roberts an explanatory list of school protocol outlining school requirements, including uniform, he told her that he would now take me to my classroom, after which a senior girl would be detailed to look after me until I knew my way around. It was almost lunchtime now but as there were no facilities for school meals in this building, I would be taken across to the college, a few streets away, where I could obtain lunch. Dinner money was to be handed to our form teacher each Monday morning and a ticket would be issued for each day of that week. Mrs. Roberts paid up, leaving me no option other than to take school dinners thereafter. Making sure that I had the bus fare home, Mrs. Roberts departed, and my school day began at last.

The headmaster then found a senior girl to assist me, instructing her to introduce me to my form teacher and then to escort me over to the college for lunch, having first obtained the necessary lunch voucher from the teacher. The girl took me along to class where Miss Robinson, the form mistress, was in the middle of a lesson; she had no idea who I was. I was acutely aware of my appearance as we entered and all heads turned towards us. My face was badly bruised and still a little swollen, and although the eye patch had by now been removed, my eye was still partly closed.

"Good heavens" she greeted us, pleasantly enough. "Whatever happened to you? Did you run into a brick wall?" The class tittered.

"I got it playing hockey." I replied.

It turned out that Miss Robinson was also the games mistress, and she showed immediate interest.

"Oh. So you're a hockey player are you?" she went on. "Where do you play?"

"No." I answered. "I got it at my old school."

"But the hockey season is only just beginning." she continued. "How do you mean?"

"I didn't know that I had passed my scholarship and went back to my old school last week." I replied.

"Oh dear!" she said, turning to the senior girl, who then informed her of the headmaster's instructions, as the class of girls looked on.

I was aware that all were neatly dressed in navy and white uniform, complete with school tie. I was wearing an ill-fitting jumper and skirt, and brown brogue shoes; theirs were black. In addition I was carrying a brown coat which had been passed on to me by Mrs. Roberts' younger sister, on my last visit to Bolton, as I had by now grown out of the one I had arrived at The Pines in twelve months earlier. Fortunately my hair, although still short, was held in place by the hair-slide.

Having made a note of my name, Miss Robinson turned back to her class and dismissed me, telling me to report back to her after lunch.

She was helpful without probing further during the afternoon, handing me various exercise books and pointing out that some of the text books were only obtainable by buying them from the college, and as individual teachers taught different lessons, they would instruct me on what exactly I needed. The other girls had already got theirs, but she felt sure that someone would share with me for the time being. She introduced me to the form prefect, explaining that I could depend on the prefect to see that I attended the correct classes. She advised me to get a school satchel as quickly as possible as I would be carrying books around with me constantly.

All in all the afternoon passed quickly and as I caught the bus back to The Pines I began to think that at last I was in the right school for me! Mrs. Roberts and Miss Somers were both waiting for me in the kitchen, eager to see how I had got on.

I filled them in as best I could. It was a two-year commercial course, and I was in a first-year class, consisting of 35 girls. There was a corresponding class of 35 pupils, also first-year, of which about half a dozen were boys; presumably boys who had shown an interest in a commercial career. None of the year's intake came from my old school, most of <u>them</u> having opted for technical courses. The next two classes in my present school contained the second and final year students. I explained that classes were split between the school Mrs. Roberts had seen that morning and the neighbouring college. The typing classes were held at the college where all the typewriters were, and we were to have a lesson the following morning. Apparently all the girls loved the typing lessons. The class prefect had helped me to compose a timetable that afternoon and this showed that shorthand, typing, French, history and geography were also on the curriculum, as well as English and mathematics. Games periods were to be arranged later; there was no P.E. I further explained that I needed books, a satchel, and most of all a school uniform.

Nothing could be done that night however, and so the three of us tried to find suitable dark clothing for the time being. There were no other shoes, I was stuck with my brown ones for now, but Mrs. Roberts assured me that she would inform Miss Norton when she returned that night, and also make sure that Matron knew what was required. She would be giving the headmaster's list to Matron the next day.

* * *

I spent the rest of the week endeavouring to make the best of everything I encountered but at first found it difficult to adjust to not having my own desk to keep my books etc. together. Of course a satchel would have made a big difference, as this was in effect, looked upon as one's 'desk' by the other students. However a satchel couldn't just be plucked out of thin air for me and it was to be the week-end before Mrs. Roberts took me into the town centre, in her own time, to get one for me. By this time I had a better idea of what was required and she made sure mine matched the other girls' in style and quality. On the same outing I was also able to obtain the obligatory school beret, and as I had already purchased the school badge, Mrs. Roberts was able to stitch it on to the beret for me before the following week commenced.

By the end of the week I had amassed quite an amount of books to be carried around with me to various classrooms in the two buildings in which we were taught, and also as I had homework to contend with I had to keep them all together en route to and from school. The satchel made life a lot easier, once it was in use. Towards the end of the week the form prefect had approached me in a responsible manner asking me if I would be getting my school uniform shortly, pointing out that I was the only girl in our form without one yet, whereas two or three of the students in the corresponding class were letting their classmates down with an untidy appearance. By this time I knew that rivalry existed between the two forms, in fact it was encouraged by the teachers, but I patiently explained that things were moving along as fast as possible. I also confided to her at this stage that I was in a children's home, and the staff were aware of what was required, but none of us had had an opportunity to do anything about it yet. The prefect was well liked and respected by all we girls and was about eighteen months older than me and had in fact been head girl at her previous school; she had a very responsible attitude. Ages in this school varied, from thirteen upwards. I was one of the younger ones.

Eventually after a few weeks everything came together. My black eye gradually faded, school uniform, including new black school shoes, and books and equipment, were obtained and I settled down in class, where all the girls were friendly. I liked all the lessons, especially the shorthand and typing, and worked hard. After a short period of trying to do homework in the kitchen, surrounded by children being bathed in the nearby bathroom etc., I was allowed each evening to sit at a table in the empty dining room to do it. I enjoyed these periods of privacy and didn't work quickly! It was to stand me in good stead at examination time.

The only thing that blighted my outlook on school now was my short hair! The hairdresser still came to The Pines once each month to cut everyone's hair. I still pleaded with her not to cut mine, explaining that I was now at a different school and I was the only one with short hair, but although she did her best to help, her hands were tied.

Most of the girls at school had attractive hairstyles, and the older ones wore make-up once they were out of uniform, so it was a big problem as far as I was concerned; I was different. It was to be about two or three months before Mrs. Roberts took matters into her own hands and approached Matron about it. Miss Norton was then instructed to let my hair grow a little longer.

This was not the first time that Mrs. Roberts had intervened on my behalf. Not receiving the original letter informing me of the scholarship gained, before school re-commenced, had caused me many problems, and she was determined to find out when and where the letter had been delivered. During my first week at the new school she had quietly waited for Matron to make her own enquiries from Miss Norton, who normally opened the post. However, not hearing anything to the contrary, she presumed that Matron had either forgotten or not bothered, and so she then asked Miss Norton if she had been aware of a letter being delivered to The Pines, addressed to Mrs. Bailey.

"Yes. A letter was delivered here several weeks ago." Miss Norton replied.

"What happened to it?" Mrs. Roberts enquired.

"I gave it back to the postman two or three days later." she answered. "We didn't have a Mrs. Bailey here and so I thought it would probably be for one of the residents in the flats next door. I have already explained to Matron." A house as large as The Pines, situated next door to us, had been converted into private apartments. The name of the house, on the gatepost, had no resemblance to The Pines.

I was present when Mrs. Roberts related the conversation to Miss Somers and saw the incredulous look that passed between them. It was followed by a bald statement that they both knew that Miss Norton had steamed open letters in the past. However it was 'water under the bridge' now.

This episode confirmed to all three of us our suspicions that Miss Norton had taken a dislike to me at an early stage of my arrival at The Pines. I personally thought that it was because I would not befriend Mary, who continued to be favoured by her. I couldn't think of any other reason for her attitude to me, as I was obedient and worked hard. Both my friends, Mrs. Roberts and Miss Somers, were, in their opinion, only trying to make sure injustice toward me did not take place. Originally they had fought my corner from the background but as time went on and they learned that I could keep my own counsel, they had discussed things more openly in front of me. Apparently I had a predecessor who had left The Pines shortly before I arrived, and they felt that she had been unfairly treated; they were not going to stand by and see the same thing happen to me.

Most of my school uniform had been obtained by Matron from various sources and paid for by Stockport Treasury. She had bought it by size only and most of it fitted reasonably well. However as winter approached it was obvious that I would need the obligatory navy school coat and the size of this could not be judged unless I was present. It was therefore arranged that she would personally take me to Manchester at the first opportunity, in order to obtain one. We went in her car; I was rather apprehensive, as she always seemed rather distant to me.

After obtaining the coat she informed me that she would hopefully be bringing me again on another occasion, to buy a dress for weekend wear. Now, purchases done, she was going to take me to see something very special indeed, and she felt sure that I would like it!

She took me to look at Princess Elizabeth's wedding dress, displayed on a model at a gallery in Manchester. Princess Elizabeth had married Prince Philip almost twelve months earlier at Westminster Abbey and the dress, having been displayed in London for several months had recently been brought to Manchester for the northern population to admire. It was encased in a very large glass display unit, situated in the centre of a room, in a fine art gallery in the town centre. Visitors were able to walk around the glass cabinet as many times as they wished. The dress was made from white satin, heavily beaded, with a beautifully beaded train laid out behind. We were both impressed.

It was quite a change for me when I was next in school to be able to describe something so unique to the other girls. Normally when they asked me what I had done over the weekend I had nothing to report! Mrs. Roberts and Miss Somers laughed when I related the event to them. They had known that Matron must have had an ulterior motive in escorting me to Manchester, but hadn't been able to work out what it was!

Chapter 20

FAMILY VISITS

I still visited my aunt from time to time on Saturday afternoons as it was preferable to staying at The Pines for the whole weekend without a break. However if either Mrs. Roberts or Miss Somers were able to include a treat for me in their own free time by taking me out with them, I jumped at the chance! Miss Somers who lived with her sister and family would sometimes take me to have tea with them and we would get back to The Pines in time for her evening shift. I enjoyed these outings enormously, as not only did it remind me what family life was like, I was also able to have normal conversations with people of approximately my own age. Miss Somers had a niece and nephew. The only other time I could talk with my contemporaries was at school.

It was more difficult for Mrs. Roberts to take me home with her on her weekly day off as she had to travel to Bolton and this interfered with my schooldays. However if she had a free Saturday afternoon she would sometimes take me shopping etc., occasionally having afternoon tea, and sometimes if she was free for the evening shift, she would take me to see a good film at the cinema. Mrs. Roberts' main hobby was sewing, much of which was done on the sewing machine housed in the attic room. In addition to making garments for herself, Miss Somers, or even her own sister at Bolton, all of which she did in her own 'off-duty' time, she also did the making and mending of household items for The Pines.

On one of my visits to my aunt, my brother Jack was at home. He explained that he would be going to visit our mother the following weekend and if I could make arrangements with the staff at The Pines, he was prepared to take me with him, as a pillion passenger on his motorcycle, and attempt to take me inside the hospital with him. He told me to wear suitably warm clothing; he would lend me some fur-lined boots and gloves to wear whilst on the motorcycle, but it was important that I endeavoured to make myself look older than I actually was, as I was supposed to wait until I was fourteen before I could visit. By now I was six months short of that age but quite tall and slim and we both thought that I could carry it off. I was elated!

Arrangements were made and I made my way to my aunt's house earlier than usual the following Saturday. Miss Somers had allowed me to borrow her outdoor coat, which was both warm and weatherproof, but would still look decent when I removed the motorcycle boots and replaced them with shoes. I did not wear ankle socks to school anymore, these having been replaced with long black stockings, so the stockings were ideal for wearing for the occasion, keeping me warm whilst on the motorcycle as well. To complete the ensemble Miss Somers lent me a bag with a shoulder strap, again which I could wear whilst en route and Mrs. Roberts fixed me up with a headscarf, which in addition to making me look more grown up, was very necessary on the motorcycle to protect my head against the wind. Motorcycle helmets were not obligatory in 1948 and Jack had supplied goggles for both of us to protect our eyes.

After giving me instructions on how to sit on the pillion seat, where to put my feet, how to hold on to his body securely, how to lean to one side when he did and how to attract his attention if I needed to stop for anything, Jack took me on a short practice run around the local streets, and at the end of this I assured him that I was perfectly happy to attempt the journey to the hospital near Preston. He told me that it would take us approximately one and a half hours, travelling through Bolton, Chorley and Preston before we arrived.

He stopped the motorcycle at a pretty spot with a nice view over a reservoir, about halfway through the journey to have a break and to ensure that I was alright.

We eventually arrived at the hospital and made ourselves look presentable before we entered, and he reminded me that I was now fourteen years of age! He warned me however that it was still possible that the staff here would not let either of us see mother if she wasn't up to receiving visitors, in which case we would leave our parcels of 'tit-bits' for her at reception and try again next month. He told me not to volunteer any information, just do as he did.

A reception desk was situated in the entrance hall, where a register of patients was being monitored by a member of staff. Visits had to be pre-booked and therefore patients would be available for their expected visitors when they arrived. We checked in without trouble and were then directed to the ballroom nearby, the doors of which were closed, with a member of staff on duty outside and another one inside to take us to the patient.

Mother was sitting alone, about half way along a row of seats situated under a window. She was dressed in a blouse and skirt, which had been provided by my aunt on a previous visit. The first thing my mind registered was that she too had been made to have her hair cut in an institutionalized bob. She was calm as she looked towards us, recognising Jack but unsure who was with him. I took off the headscarf and held out my arms as we approached and she jumped to her feet as she realised who I was. She smiled and hugged me, at the same time looking beyond me for Clifford. We were surrounded by scores of people, both visitors and patients, and she must have thought that he was in the crowd, as she associated us both together. Jack had to explain that only two visitors were allowed, not daring to mention that Clifford was not old enough to visit. He assured her that he would try to bring him next time!

She was obviously pleased to see us but we had not really taken into account that I had changed a lot since she last saw me and although she held both my hands as I sat opposite her on a chair placed there by Jack, conversation was a bit stilted. I had previously been warned by Jack not to cry, as this would upset her and spoil future visits as it had already done in the past, but of course I couldn't help feeling sad, seeing my mother so vulnerable. Her manner was hesitant and her eyes lacked lustre. I had always been used to her being in control over me and I recognised that that wasn't there any more.

As we started to unpack our gifts for her we were approached by a nurse who, after enquiring if everything was alright, suggested that perhaps we would be better off in the ward where it would be much quieter. We gladly took up her offer and followed her out of the room and up a corridor, passing through many doors, which had to be unlocked and locked again, until we reached mother's ward. We were all more relaxed by now and made an effort to be cheerful whilst we unpacked the items, sitting around a wicker table, on comfortable chairs, in an adjoining corridor. Aunt Edith had sent the usual basic items mother requested every month and Mrs. Roberts had baked some nice cakes and scones for me to give to her and also fixed me up with writing paper and envelopes, as she knew how much I longed for regular letters from my mother.

We talked and she showed us the kitchen adjoining the ward, where she was allowed to make tea etc., and told us of the library and other recreational rooms, pointing out however that the doors were always locked and she was a virtual prisoner. She complained that brother Bill had not been to see her for a long time and as he was named as her next of kin he was the one who was supposed to approach the staff for a progress report. She felt well enough to come out of hospital into his care, but he was not keeping in touch.

"Look at her." she said, pointing to me. "She's growing up and I'm missing it!"

Jack did his best to console her, assuring her that he would get in touch with Bill and tell him to visit, while I looked on with an aching throat, longing to tell her how much I loved her. All three of us shed tears when she looked Jack straight in the eye and said: "I don't want to die in here

Jack." He promised that he would not let that happen, and he meant it.

As the afternoon drew to a close it was time to leave, and again I had been forewarned by Jack not to prolong the departure as it always ended in tears. I had tried to tell my mother about my school life but she didn't really listen; when I was talking she spent most of the time just looking at me with a wistful expression. Instinct told me not to talk about The Pines as I realised that she still thought Clifford and I were at least in touch with each other. I didn't inform her that I hardly ever saw him.

We kept to safe subjects when we were leaving, making much of my first ride on Jack's motorcycle and how cold it was! When she started to cry and cling to me, a nurse was on hand to comfort her and help her with her possessions, as another one unlocked the doors; we were able to wave to each other through glass partitions as Jack and I departed down the corridor. Once we were out of sight I let the tears fall as Jack put his arm across my shoulders. She <u>was</u> a prisoner, but why? She had seemed perfectly normal to me. I realised at that point that her situation was far worse than mine.

Jack was tight-lipped as we made our way back to the motorcycle after checking-out with the registrar. From the few words exchanged between us I could tell that he was very angry with brother Bill. It had really been Bill's turn to visit mother on this occasion but when he had let my aunt know that he wouldn't be going in this instance, Jack had decided to utilise the allowed visit by taking me. He told me that he would make sure that Bill went next time! A month must have seemed a long time for my mother.

We stopped for a snack on the way back before he delivered me to the front door at The Pines, as previously arranged. Miss Norton was on duty and had reserved a meal for me. I ate it in the kitchen, surrounded by children being bathed.

Chapter 21

LETTERS

A short time after I started at commercial school it was decided that I should have some spending money of my own each week, with which to buy treats at school or on my weekend excursions, and a small amount of money was given to me, usually by Miss Norton, every Saturday. Until this happened Mrs. Roberts or Miss Somers usually gave me the odd shilling or two, from their own pockets. I was careful with the money, allowing myself treats at school when most of the other girls had them, but I saved as much as I could so that I would have money for things that I really wanted. I also wanted to buy Christmas presents, especially for my mother and Clifford.

As Christmas 1948 approached I was in a fairly settled frame of mind. At the end of October I had been to see my mother, I liked my new school and was doing well, having come 24th in class tests at half term, an improvement of eleven places. By Christmas I was placed at 16th, and it also felt good to have a bit of money to call my own.

I had not been able to visit my mother again, as November and December visits were taken up with my two brothers and my aunt, but I made sure that I sent her some writing paper and envelopes around Christmas time and an accompanying letter telling her that I had been thinking of getting her a pendant on a chain. I hadn't been able to find a suitable one in time for Christmas but would most likely be able to manage it for her birthday in February. I thought she would be able to wear a pendant and chain every day and think of me. Jack and my aunt both made sure that my mother received gifts at Christmas and told me that she was well.

I bought suitable little gifts for Mrs. Roberts and Miss Somers and accompanied both of them to carol services at different times and venues. Miss Somers took me to the Salvation Army citadel and Mrs. Roberts took me to a church service in Stockport. I enjoyed these outings tremendously.

Mrs. Roberts was on duty on Boxing Day, when Jack turned up on his motorcycle with a present for me. It was a lovely purse made from pigskin leather, soft and pliable, complete with extra compartments for notes and suchlike. I was delighted. He also had a present for Clifford, which he was about to deliver. He asked Mrs. Roberts for directions to get there and enquired whether or not she thought that he would be allowed to see Clifford to personally give him the present. She felt sure Miss Jackson would allow a few minutes and suggested that he took me along as well. He was happy to do so and I was delighted, hurriedly donning warm clothes, complete with headscarf! I had met Miss Jackson three or four weeks earlier when she visited The Pines and I was introduced to her.

Thornleigh was situated at the other side of Stockport from The Pines but it didn't take us long to get there on the motorcycle. We rang the bell at the front door, which was opened by Miss Jackson. Jack explained who he was and politely asked if he could see Clifford and as she shook her head, at the same time holding out her hand for the parcel, I made myself known.

"Hello Miss Jackson" was all I could think of on the spur of the moment, desperate that she would let us see him.

"Is it Mavis?" was her reply, and I thought for a moment she would relent as I nodded. She had obviously mistaken me at first for a possible girlfriend of Jack's in my borrowed headscarf.

"Does Miss Norton know you are here?"

I truthfully told her that she didn't, but Mrs. Roberts did!

Jack informed her that Mrs. Roberts had given permission for me to go with him, on the off-chance that we might see Clifford and give him a present.

She wouldn't budge, saying that the boys were still eating lunch.

When Jack offered to wait outside until lunch was over, and even though it must have been obvious from my pleading eyes that I wanted to see him, she still would not relent, saying only that it was not fair on the other boys. Jack handed over the gift and we left. What hurt most of all was that we were on the doorstep and Clifford, a few yards away, was not aware of it.

I think Mrs. Roberts was quite disgusted when we got back to The Pines and told her.

* * *

Miss Somers had arranged to go with her sister and family to a pantomime on New Year's Eve. at Stockport Theatre Royal and asked me if I would like to go along with them, as there was a spare ticket. Of course I was delighted to go, and it was arranged that after the pantomime we would all attend the midnight service to be held at the Salvation Army citadel. From there we would go to stay at the home of Miss Somers' sister and family overnight and I could share a room with her niece Jean.

I had a wonderful evening; the pantomime was Cinderella and I recognised the name of the Dame as being someone my mother used to think was very amusing. I was very keen to let Jean and her relations know that I too used to have family outings and I remembered seeing the comedian, Harry Korris some years back. Of course it was also quite an experience for me to see in the New Year at midnight, and I went to sleep that night in Jean's room feeling very happy. I was sure it wouldn't be long now before my mother was better and we would all be together again.

The next day, back at The Pines, I wrote to my mother, telling her about the previous evening's events and she in turn sent me the following letter, which I received just after I started back at school for the spring term. It was written in pencil on the blue writing paper I had sent to her at Christmas and each page was carefully numbered.

C.M.H. Ward 9,
Main,
Whittingham.
Nr. Preston.
Monday Jan. 10th 1949.

My Dear Mavis,

Many thanks for your welcome letter, sorry I have not answered it before now. Well Mavis I hope you are right and that I will be home before you come again.

I was pleased to know you also went to a pantomime called Cinderella, fancy Harry Koris being in it, I am glad you enjoyed it. My word you were having a late night weren't you? Still it was new years eve and I always used to stay up and listen to the bells, so did your Grandma (my mother), it was her birthday yesterday, 9th January.

Well Mavis if you can't get a pendant it doesn't matter, just send me a bit of something, I don't mind, that is if I am still here and it looks now as though I will be but I do hope I keep as well as I am now. I have asked the Matron if I could go in the laundry and she said she will have to see.

Well Mavis love I don't think there is much more to say now only that I hope to hear from you again very soon. Give our Clifford my love and I hope he is keeping well. I suppose I won't know him when I do see him. Well I must close my letter now love so all my love to you as ever.

I am your loving and <u>devoted</u> mother.

XXXXXXXXXXXXXXXX

P.S. Thank you for the stamped addressed envelope.

Goodnight Dear.

I could hardly wait to show Mrs. Roberts my letter, as I had often complained to her that I didn't understand why my mother was in the hospital, and when I had been to see her she had seemed perfectly normal. She had done her best to help, and encouraged me to keep up my spirits, but I always felt that she had a different opinion.

At times she had said that if my mother didn't need treatment she wouldn't be in that hospital and there was no quick remedy, but I didn't agree with her. In my heart I knew that it was because none of our relations were willing to look after her. I also felt that my mother realised this and that was why she always wanted to see brother Bill.

However I persuaded Mrs. Roberts to read the letter, even though she was reluctant to do so, and watched her face as I waited for a response, excitedly triumphant as she told me that there was nothing wrong with my mother if she could write a letter like that. I knew I was right and her acknowledgement meant everything to me!

I sent mother the pendant for her birthday, February 2nd, and received the following letter in reply.

C.M.H.
Ward 14 (Main)
Whittingham,
Nr. Preston.
Monday, Feb. 6th 1949.

Dear Mavis,

Many thanks for your lovely birthday present, also your card, both of which I received on the morning of my birthday, I also received two cards and a nice pair of stockings. The stockings were from auntie Edie, also a card, the other card was from our Jack. Our Bill never sent me a card. I am feeling very well just now and I am glad because I should be coming home soon.

Well Mavis you asked me if I received the photographs. Yes love I got them quite safely and they are very good ones especially our Clifford's. I wouldn't have thought that he would have taken such a good one. Yours is absolutely a knock out as usual.

Well I haven't much to tell you only that I hope it won't be long before we are together once more. Oh yes Mavis, I was so glad you sent me a writing pad, it is so useful, also the stamps.

I haven't much time to say any more now but perhaps I will write more next time, so I will say ta ta for now and all my love to you and Clifford, also Jack.

I remain your ever loving

Mother XXXXXXXXXXXXXXX

P.S.Will you please ask our Jack and your auntie Edie if they will bring me a tin of milk when they bring my bit of tea next time (instead of sugar) and some butter and a tin of treacle or something like that.

.

Shortly after writing this letter my mother applied for and obtained, a job in the laundry at the hospital. She was paid five old shillings per week for this strenuous work, money that could then be spent in the hospital shop. My mother however, having had a taste of the freedom going to and from the laundry through the hospital grounds, had other ideas. She saved most of the money, paid weekly, for the four or five weeks she worked, and when the time was right she simply walked out of the grounds, with her money, and made her way to Blackpool, by bus.

The first my aunt, or any of us, knew about this, was when the local police turned up at my aunt's home looking for my mother. They explained that she had absconded and they would expect to be informed if any of her relatives were to see her or hear from her. I was blissfully ignorant of what was happening and only found out the next time I visited my aunt.

On arrival at Blackpool, my mother, remembering the address of a friend of aunt Edith's, made her way there. When the friend and her husband had finished listening to her story, they covertly telephoned the hospital; the staff in turn contacted the police. My mother's freedom was short-lived. Of course the couple couldn't possibly assess the nature of my mother's mental state, but were to quote their own story to aunt Edith at a later date.

She had taken tea with them, and they had each enquired about various friends and family. They confirmed that her conversation had been rational until the police arrived, at which point she had cried out accusingly to them that they had betrayed her. She had not gone quietly; shouting and screaming that there was nothing wrong with her and she only wanted to see her children! She pleaded with the couple to just let her stay for a few days, but of course they could not.

It was two or three weeks later before I heard this dreadful news. I had gone to visit my aunt on my usual Saturday excursion and was determined to make sure that I was included somehow in the next visit, only to be informed that there were to be no more visits for a while. She then related the whole sorry story to me and of course I wept, thinking how everything seemed to go wrong for my mother.

She had done the worst possible thing she could have done by breaking the trust of the hospital staff. In addition of course the personnel concerned were admonished for their lack of foresight and so it was inevitable that she would be punished, if not officially, then by the staff making life difficult for her. All privileges were withdrawn, including visits for a time, and in response to her non co-operative attitude, treatment was stepped up. This included electric shock treatment, straight jacket in a padded cell, and a locked ward at all times. Fortunately I was not aware of this atrocious treatment at the time.

As far as I know, Mrs. Roberts was not aware of the situation either until I informed her that there were to be no more visits for a while. Her face showed pain, shock and incredulity as she endeavoured to comfort me as I wept in her arms. I kept insisting that my mother was not mentally ill and eventually she agreed. She once again said that if my mother had made her way to Blackpool, travelling over unfamiliar territory, finding an unfamiliar address and saving the money with which to do it, then she was not mentally unfit. She tried to comfort me, telling me that surely this would go down on her records to show that she was capable of looking after herself and her children, what we had to do now was to give my mother time to calm down and then she could be re-assessed. In the meantime I had to bide my time and work hard at school and try not to worry. She would help me all she could.

Chapter 22

FOURTEEN

True to her word Mrs. Roberts did her best to make sure that I was kept as busy as possible during the following weeks. I continued to work hard both at school and with my homework and managed to increase my position in class by another two places when we took Easter exams. I began to realise that my homework dedication was paying off as I practiced shorthand outlines, French phrases and commercial studies. My main reason for putting in so much homework was so that I could have a little privacy in the dining room during the evenings. There was a period when Miss Norton brought Mary into the dining room, ostensibly to help me with my homework, but probably to check up on what I was doing. I couldn't refuse to let her in but she quickly got bored with the little actions of help I was able to offer her and after a few days or so didn't bother to come in. I also wrote to my mother occasionally during my homework periods. Her replies were spasmodic but on my birthday at the beginning of May I did receive a card with fourteen kisses on it. This lifted my spirits as it proved to me that she was thinking of me and remembering what age I had become. At the time I overlooked how it must have saddened her.

About Easter time Matron once more took me shopping in Manchester, and this time I finished up with three new dresses and a Sunday top-coat. I was growing fast, and apart from my school uniform there was nothing at The Pines to fit me. I had long since grown out of the American clothes and until the new ones were bought for me I constantly borrowed skirts and tops from Miss Somers who was the same size as me.

Both Miss Somers and Mrs. Roberts took me home with them whenever schooldays allowed and with my new outfits I began to feel that I could hold my own, both with their families and also with my contemporaries from school. My one disappointment however was my shoes! Nobody's shoes would fit me and so I was forced to wear my school brogues for all occasions. I had never had dainty feet and felt that the laced-up brogues made my feet look enormous.

Mrs. Roberts solved this problem by treating me to a new pair of shoes for weekend wear, for my birthday at the beginning of May, and I was allowed to choose them myself from a town centre shop. Miss Somers came with us and afterwards we all had tea at a cinema restaurant. It was a lovely day for me.

* * *

At this time I did not go to my aunt's house quite so often on Saturday afternoons, preferring instead to be taken out by one or the other of my friendly housemothers. In addition once I reached the age of fourteen, I was allowed to go to the cinema on Saturday evenings by myself, when they couldn't accompany me due to shift duties, and also of course they each had their own social calendar.

One Saturday afternoon, when Mrs. Roberts was on duty, Jack turned up on his motorcycle to see me. He had come with the news that visits to my mother were to be reinstated and asked if I would like to go; he suggested a date for the future. As he was about to leave and we were both saying goodbye to him at the front door Mrs. Roberts asked him what he thought my mother's prognosis was. Did he think she would ever recover enough to come out of the hospital? He shook his head.

I was hovering in the background, stunned to witness what I looked upon as this act of betrayal, and drew a sharp incredulous intake of breath, looking at him in horror. With a quick turn I fled down the hall, up the stairs, and into the toilet compartment at the top, situated next to Mrs. Roberts' bedroom, where I sobbed incessantly. Mrs. Roberts pleaded with me to come out and when I wouldn't, she came in; the door could not be locked. She helped me on to the landing and we sat on the stairs and she cuddled me. I tried to tell her that Jack was wrong; my mother was well when I last saw her, and in her letters she always talked about us all eventually being back together again.

She cried with me and blamed herself for asking for Jack's opinion in front of me, saying that it <u>was</u> only an opinion and none of us really knew the extent of mother's illness. The truth was she had her own agenda, unknown to me at the time, and was only trying to find out what the future had in store for <u>me</u>.

When my sobs subsided a little, in an effort to comfort me she confided that she often thought I could do with a little mothering myself, and asked me if I could look upon her as my mother for the time being. She was of course already a trusted friend to me and so this wasn't a real problem until she suggested that I addressed her as 'mother' when we were on our own. I knew that I could never give her that title and she probably felt my body stiffen at the suggestion.

"I don't want to completely take your mother's place." she said hurriedly, "But if I am to look upon you as my daughter, Mrs. Roberts sounds a bit formal, don't you think?"

I could see her point but was too upset to work out the implications as I promised to try to remember to refer to her as my mother when possible. She sent me to lie down on her bed.

Nothing more on the matter was discussed between us for a few weeks after that. I accompanied my aunt on the bus to visit my mother at the pre-arranged date, and Jack met us at the hospital, having travelled alone on his motorcycle. We were going to take it in turns to go to mother's ward but the staff let us all in together. The visit did not go well. My mother was tearful most of the time, pleading with my aunt to take her home. Jack had to explain to her that she was not fully recovered yet, but he had to agree with her when she pointed out that it was all that could be expected, spending all her days locked in that place; conversation with other patients was not stimulating!

* * *

The routine of morning cleaning, followed by daily school life, went on for me as usual in the latter part of that school year, 1949, and at examination time I once more crept up the ladder of class position to 9th place. I did not have any one special friend at school but was a member of a group of four and we were all competitive. In our little group, one friend was placed above me at the end of term and the other two were not far behind.

Everyone was getting excited about parents' evening. Some of the girls in the year above us were due to leave school with distinction at that time and we were all expected to attend the leaving ceremony, to be held in the college assembly hall, and also to encourage our parents to accompany us in support of the school as a whole. It would be a rehearsal for when it would be our turn, the following year!

I just took it for granted that although I would do my best to attend, I would be on my own. Mrs. Roberts had other ideas. Nothing was going to keep her from being present and being introduced to my friends and their parents. In the end Miss Somers went along as well as company for her, as of course I had to sit with the other students. In the little social gatherings after the ceremony I introduced them both to my friends, who all knew that I was in a children's home, but I could not bring myself to use the word 'parent'. Afterwards we all three went to a little café nearby for coffee etc. It was full of other students and their families.

My school report reflected my hard work throughout the year and I was even congratulated by Matron. Also at this time I learned that Clifford had passed his eleven-plus examination and would be going to a top grammar school. I asked if I could see him and learned that we would be seeing each other when all we children went on holiday together in August. This time we were to go to Squires Gate Holiday

Camp, near Blackpool. Mrs. Roberts and Miss Norton were to represent the The Pines staff, the other homes would have their own complement.

* * *

The holiday at Squires Gate was much more successful than the previous year's had been. Games were organised for the children and those of us who were old enough could swim and splash about in the swimming pool. Poolside competitions were organised by the camp staff and beach games entered into by we girls and boys under our own steam. Meals were taken in the dining hall, and although we filled many tables, we were treated exactly the same as the other guests. In fact one of our waitresses who lived locally, and was engaged to be married, became friendly with Mrs. Roberts and used to joke with her that she was practising on we children prior to having a bunch of her own!

Clifford and I spent quite a lot of time together, taking pleasure in competing with each other, as we had done in earlier days, and I could see that even though he was of slender build, he looked better than I had ever seen him. Many of the other girls and boys were reconciled with their siblings for the first time in years and everyone, including the staff, took delight in this. When Mrs. Roberts attended a function on behalf of the smaller children, I went along with her to help. In her free time she took me into Blackpool to see the sights. On one occasion all we girls and boys who were old enough had a couple of hours at Blackpool fairground, trying out the rides and roundabouts etc.Altogether it was a most welcome change for all of us.

* * *

Before Clifford started grammar school in September 1949, Jack and my aunt sought and obtained permission to take him with them on their next visit to my mother. They were hoping to at least let them both have a short time together by pretending he was fourteen years old if necessary. Of course I couldn't go at this time but my aunt related events to me at a later date.

The ploy of sneaking him in with them had not been as successful as it was when I went on my first visit. I had looked older than my thirteen years, whilst he looked the age he was, just twelve.

At Reception they were warned that he was not really allowed to visit at his age, but because of the distance travelled, they would make an exception and allow a few minutes, under supervision.

My mother had probably been told that her young son was on his way to see her and positioned herself as far down the corridor as she could, standing behind the locked glass-panelled door at the far end. She and Clifford could see each other as the doors were unlocked one by one, and the little group made their way toward her.

It was a disaster. By the time they reached her she was on the point of collapse, her hands sliding down the glass as she struggled to keep upright.

"My baby. My baby" she cried. "Come here. Let me hold you."

But because of her distraught condition the two nurses on either side of the door, shook their heads at each other and the door remained locked. Mother crying on one side,

Clifford also crying, on the other, their hands and faces up against the glass.

The visitors were told to leave as mother was helped away in the opposite direction, resulting in no visiting that day and instructions not to bring anyone under the age of fourteen in future.

Of course this episode left its mark on all concerned.

Chapter 23

FREE TIME

School began again in September after the long summer break and I realised that the time had passed reasonably quickly, incorporating the holiday at Blackpool and a few days spent with Mrs. Roberts at her home in Bolton. She took me out and about and I enjoyed my sense of freedom. I was given the run of her mother's home, introduced to more friends and relatives, and accompanied her to church and various other functions. Her mother was actually her widowed step-mother, her own mother having died a quarter of a century earlier and her father had remarried. Their daughter (Mrs. Roberts' half sister), nearly a generation younger, lived nearby and also befriended me. Like Miss Somers, she too wore the same size of clothes as I did and constantly gave or lent to me odd items. I always felt a little sad when the time came to leave.

However, going back to school was quite pleasurable for me and I looked forward to seeing my friends again and meeting the demands of a new form structure, in what was to be my final year at school. In this final year, we were to spend more time in the college itself improving our typing skills and generally acquiring more commercial experience, including elementary book-keeping. I loved it.

Being in the college building more often meant that we could take advantage of various social activities from time to time. For example there was a room equipped with table tennis facilities, which we could make use of in our lunch break. It was highly sought after however and the custom was to find a partner and reserve a table in advance. We usually managed to play about twice each week, other students also taking a turn.

The college was quite large of course, accommodating many senior students, both full-time and part-time, and open to the public in general. I was not street-wise and when I left my lovely pig-skin purse containing my money in my coat pocket in the cloakroom, it was stolen. I was more upset about the purse than the money, even though I had to walk home that evening. Months later the purse was found, along with several others, emptied and hidden in the lavatory-flushing cistern. It was ruined of course.

Situated next door to the college was an all-girls grammar school which was in fact the school that June, my friend of two or three years earlier when I lived at home with my mother, had passed the eleven-plus entrance examination for. Being in close proximity now meant that from time to time we encountered each other in our free time. I think she was genuinely pleased to see me again but we each had a new set of friends and only swapped pleasantries. I was pleased to note however that her school uniform only differed from mine in colour. I knew she would tell my old neighbours that she had seen me, looking good.

Sometimes during our lunch break I would saunter into the nearby town centre, along with my friends, and we would spend time listening to records in Woolworth's store and chatting to boys of our own age, most of whom attended the local technical college. I loved the freedom of choosing where I went and with whom, my only disappointment being that when the girls were making arrangements to see each other away from school I always had to refuse. In time they came to accept this and I didn't have to think up excuses. On one of my excursions, walking along with my friends, I came face to face with an old neighbour, the one in whose garden my mother had left our possessions in the tin trunk. She recognised me immediately, and her eyes filled with tears when she saw me. We had a short conversation but I did not mention the thought uppermost in my mind, regarding the trunk and nor did she. Before we parted she stressed how pleased she was to see me, especially looking so well, and wished me all the best for the future. During our conversation she had asked about my mother and also confirmed that she knew I now attended college.

* * *

I continued with my homework every weekday evening and was rewarded with coming in at 6th place at the half term exams. I was especially pleased at this because I had to increase my shorthand and typing speeds at college only, as I had nothing to practice with during my homework periods. Book-keeping and other subjects <u>were</u> swotted up on for homework; as I have already said, it was preferable to sitting in the kitchen with the other girls, most of whom were still two or three years younger than me. An older girl would sometimes come to stay with us for short periods but it was rare.

On Saturdays if nothing else was on offer I occasionally went to visit my aunt, but quite often I would find out what time the main film started at one of the town centre cinemas and organise myself into catching the relevant bus at the top of the tree-lined road. If the film was certified 'A' for adults, I would ask someone suitable going into the cinema at the same time, to take me in with them. This was common practice in those days and was what I had been instructed to do by the staff. An adult certificate at the time usually meant that the film was a murder mystery or included an extra marital relationship.

One evening, queuing for the performance to begin, I asked a young couple if I could go in with them and they were quite happy to accommodate me but did not want me to sit with them. Once inside they made their way to the back of the cinema and I chose a seat about halfway down. When the lights came on at the interval I was aware of a man sitting on the row in front of me, to my right. He was positioned so that he was able to keep giving me sidelong glances and this made me feel uncomfortable. I was relieved when the lights were dimmed again and the film began. I kept a wary eye on him but he did not move from his seat.

At the end of the film I made my way outside, knowing that the bus-stop was immediately adjacent to the cinema in a well lit area. By now it was after ten o-clock but the buses were frequent, catering for the emptying cinemas. I was crestfallen when he joined me but consoled myself with the thought that many buses with different destinations stopped there. However when he began to make light conversation with me, not being experienced enough to be rude to him, I felt obliged to answer. As my bus approached I bade him goodnight, saying that this was the bus I needed but he followed me on board, saying that he too was travelling on the same bus. I did not go to the upper deck, as I would normally have done but sat just inside, near to the conductor. The man sat nearby and continued to talk to both the conductor and me in a friendly manner, giving me no cause to ask for assistance from the conductor. He looked to be about mid-twenties in age and reasonably well dressed and spoken.

My thoughts were racing as he got off the bus behind me. All I had to do now was cross the busy main road but then I would be in the tree-lined road where The Pines was situated. That was the problem; it was a long dark road. A telephone kiosk was situated on the main road and I thought about ringing Miss Somers who was on duty alone, but how could she help? She couldn't leave all the children alone in the house while she came to escort me home! I would just have to get rid of the man somehow. I stopped walking whilst still in the well-lit area and attempted further small talk, trying to think of a plan.

Eventually I saw an elderly couple walking their dog, coming towards us, and when they turned into my road I made a hasty decision to follow close on their heels. However, although I felt that they were aware of my presence I could not bring myself to ask for their help and the man was still silently following me. On reaching the entrance to The Pines grounds I stopped and the couple carried on down the road. I knew that I was now in deep trouble, having placed myself in an even worse position, as I still had the long dark tree-lined driveway to negotiate.

He started to verbally put pressure on me at that point. I can't remember all the conversation but when he began to talk about a recent murder of a young woman, which had taken place in the park near to my old school I began to be really frightened.

Suddenly out of the darkness I saw a figure running down the road towards us and realised it was a girl of about fourteen who had recently been admitted to The Pines for two or three weeks whilst her mother went into hospital. She too had been allowed to visit relations on that particular evening. When she saw me standing talking to someone she took to be a friend, she hesitated and then quickly turned around to head back the way she had come. I was speechless with fright by this time and could hardly remember her name, to call out to her.

"Winifred" I managed to shout at last. "Winifred, come on, let's go in, we're late!"

She turned around then and hurried towards us, attempting to carry on up the drive alone. Needless to say I joined her and we ran as fast as we could up the long path.

Miss Somers could immediately tell from my expression that all was not well as she answered the door- bell to us and as I blurted out my story she locked all the doors, telling Winifred to see herself into bed as she wanted to talk to me.

"Why didn't you 'phone me from the kiosk?" she asked.

"Because I knew you wouldn't be able to leave the children." I replied. She had no further answer to that, so I never found out whether or not she <u>would</u> have left them alone.

Both Mrs. Roberts and Miss Somers asked me to remember all that I had told my unwanted companion. Had I talked about the other girls at The Pines? Had I told him that there were no men in residence? Did I tell him that I regularly went out alone? I did my best to answer but the questions were far too meaningful for me to see the implications at that age and the whole episode resulted in them being more nervous than I was. It was a while before they encouraged me to go out alone at night again.

Chapter 24

FRIENDSHIPS

Mrs. Roberts did her best to make life interesting for me and took me home with her whenever she could. She did not want me to concentrate only on my school work, although everyone was very pleased with my progress. The trouble was that there were no facilities to engage in hobbies at The Pines. Even though I loved reading and would happily have gone to the library several times a week, as I had done in my earlier childhood, there was nowhere at The Pines for me to get some privacy. If Miss Norton wasn't around I could sometimes sit in the staff sitting room with a book in the evening, when all jobs were finished, but this had to be kept under wraps to avoid confrontation. The only other alternative was to do my homework in the empty dining room. It was a stark room at night, with a harsh light, and of course I sat at a table on a dining chair. Nevertheless it was preferable to sitting alone on a church pew in the empty kitchen, listening to the loud ticking of the clock situated high on the tiled walls. Once, Miss Norton came to me and pointed out that if I were to look at the clock as well as listen to it, I could actually see the minute hand jump from digit to digit!

Miss Somers, knowing my fondness for table tennis, made arrangements for me to attend a youth activity centre at the Salvation Army citadel on one or two occasions. Unfortunately the citadel was situated near to her home, completely across town, needing two buses to get there. This meant that I had to be accompanied and as the centre operated Saturday evenings, this was not ideal for Miss Somers. She much preferred to go to the Sunday evening service and found it difficult to arrange her shifts at The Pines to accommodate both evenings. However I enjoyed the occasions when I managed to get there and Miss Somers would always make sure I had one of her better outfits to borrow, so that I would not feel out of place. I began to get to know the other youngsters and as she also took me to the Sunday services whenever possible I looked forward to their company.

Another kindly action these two women introduced at The Pines was to make sure we working girls were supplied with a tray of teacups and a jug of hot tea, first thing at morning when we were making beds and polishing the floors of the dormitories. This was really welcome as winter approached that year, as we continued to do our chores every morning before breakfast and school. The tray was first introduced when Miss Norton was away for the weekend and so it was already established when she returned. Mary of course was included in our group and benefited as we did.

* * *

At school, competition was still high on the agenda as we headed for Christmas exams. We were all aware that this was our last year at school and our future careers were at stake. However I began to think that having attained 6th place at half term, that was probably as high as I could manage. Several of the girls were older and cleverer than I, some of them having already completed French courses and such like before even starting at commercial school. I didn't mind, I was comfortable with my position, and of course when we all compared notes after exams, before we were marked, it seemed to me that many of them had put on an extra spurt of dedication at this time.

Eventually it was mid-December and the marks were out. Miss Robinson was still our form mistress, having moved with us from first year, and as she assembled us at our desks to give us our positions attained, we were all waiting with bated breath. She tried to be as informal as possible at this time, as she was addressing young people on the verge of adulthood, and we were all sitting in a relaxed manner.

"Over-all, the marks attained are very good." she began. " Some of you could do better, but that's life! Your life. It's up to you to make something of it."

We sat twiddling our thumbs, willing her to get on with it!

"I will read aloud everyone's class position before handing each girl a written report, but I will begin by announcing the first five in reverse order." she continued.

I listened attentively. There was just a possibility that I had managed to increase my position from 6th at half term to 5th here and now. However my hopes were dashed when she read another girl's name out, and as I had mentally put the top three girls in the order I expected them to be placed, fourth position was my very last hope. When yet another name and congratulations were announced for 4th place, I knew I must have come sixth again. At least I fervently hoped I had not dropped at all. My attention wandered. Miss Robinson was speaking again.

"Now the next one is the one I am particularly pleased about," she said. "Because this girl came into this school as an 'also ran'. In other words she very nearly didn't make it at all! However she has worked extremely hard and certainly deserves to be placed in third position. And that girl is Mavis."

Even though I had half-heartedly listened to this build-up, I had no idea it was to be me and I looked up stunned as Miss Robinson led the class in congratulatory clapping.

I could hardly believe it. I had not worked particularly hard with my homework these last few weeks but I usually obtained good marks in class.

Obviously I was delighted and my friends sitting near to me seemed pleased also, giving me a ' thumbs up' approval sign.

The next name to be read out was one of my close friends whom I had never managed to overtake and no-one was surprised when she came second and the class prefect who was extremely clever, came first.

Miss Robinson, on discovering my circumstances very early on in my school career, had taken more than a passing interest in me. She lived near to The Pines and sometimes we would find ourselves on the same bus going to school at morning. We were always polite to each other but of course I didn't want to arrive at school accompanied by Miss Robinson on a regular basis. She did ask me a few questions about how I came to be at The Pines, when we first found ourselves travelling together, and one time she asked me if I had been there when the little girl was knocked down on the main road. I didn't know anything about this incident so she didn't enlarge upon it, but I was later told by Miss Somers that before I arrived one of the younger girls had darted into the road on her way to school and had tragically been killed. The accident happened directly in front of Miss Robinson's house and after telephoning for an ambulance, she had given first aid to the child. It was a very sad occurrence at the home and thereafter the children were always formed into a 'crocodile' column, accompanied by an adult.

* * *

After we had obtained our exam results and joined in Christmas celebrations at school it was time to break for the holiday period. I knew that I would be attending carol services again and the usual activities would take place at The Pines but more than anything I wanted to see my mother. By now I had been told by my aunt about Clifford's visit to her and how it had gone disastrously wrong, and I felt that now more than ever she would want a visit from me. I asked for permission to go to see my aunt, as lone excursions in the dark had been denied me for several weeks. I was allowed to go in daylight however, with instructions to either get accompanied back to The Pines or make sure it was still daylight when I returned. However, when I arrived at my aunt's house it was to find no-one at home. Jack and my aunt had gone to see my mother without me. They didn't know I would be turning up of course and were only playing safe by not inviting me to go with them until they had ascertained for themselves how my mother had reacted to the previous visit. However I was very disappointed, as I knew it would be a full month before I got another opportunity and by then we would be into the year 1950.

* * *

Christmas arrived and the usual routine took place. This was my third Christmas at The Pines and I had become accustomed to viewing it as a non-event from my point of view. Small presents had been exchanged with my friends at school before the holiday began and apart from going shopping with Mrs. Roberts just prior to Christmas and buying each other a present, I didn't think there would be any other surprise in store for me. However there was one; shortly before Christmas, a table was erected in the attic playroom suitable for table tennis for we older girls. Equipment was also provided. This was warmly received by all of us as of course the half dozen or so girls slightly younger than I, who had lived at The Pines for several years longer than I had, were now approaching their teens and had moved into secondary school. They too needed activity to stimulate them. None of them were familiar with table tennis, as I was, but at least it was something to engage in.

The staff took it in turns to spend a few days with their families during the Christmas holiday period and Mrs. Roberts took me with her when she went home, where I joined in the family parties, especially arranged at a time to coincide with her being at home and able to attend. These parties were held at her mother's house, with various relatives and their families congregating to celebrate. Mrs.

Roberts and her sister organised the food, consisting of many delicacies, the like of which I had never seen. In addition there were Christmas crackers, a beautifully arranged table with a small gift for everyone, and after we had eaten we played family games and sang songs around the piano. This then was family life and I was made to feel most welcome.

Chapter 25

BED REST

As New Year dawned I was in Bolton with Mrs. Roberts and her family and we had all enjoyed the recent celebrations. It was time to go back to school for the remainder of my education at day school, approximately six months.

Before the starting date arrived however, I began to feel unwell with a severe sore throat. Nothing seemed to soothe it and I quickly developed a high temperature and was confined to bed, feeling quite ill. After a day or so the doctor was called and this resulted in my going into isolation hospital for several days. The diagnosis was quinsy or sceptic tonsillitis. I think I was quite ill, not really being aware of my surroundings at times. However I remember Jack came to visit me as I lay in my isolation bed but I was only allowed to see him through the glass partition; he had been made to wear a sterilised gown for the visit. Mrs. Roberts also visited me.

Eventually I was allowed out of hospital and stayed away from school for a further week or so. During this period a bed was again made up for me in the attic which resulted in my being able to read books whilst recovering, after which I was allowed to go back to school, later than my contemporaries of course; I was glad to be back and eager to get on with my new lessons.

* * *

Periodically all the children were examined by a doctor. This usually took place on a Saturday morning in the dining room, the children going in one by one, usually accompanied by Miss Norton. Occasionally however the doctor was called to examine just one or two girls if the staff thought anyone had a health problem. Some of the girls had lifetime problems such as asthma or ongoing results of physical abuse and Margaret, the girl with the beautiful copper-coloured hair, coped all her life with the fact that her heart muscle was situated on the right-hand side of her body instead of in the normal position. Apparently, this discovery had first been made by a startled trainee-doctor, when Margaret was being examined prior to being admitted to The Pines, and he couldn't find her heartbeat. "Try the other side then," his senior had advised. "It's got to be somewhere!"

Shortly after I came out of hospital, Miss Norton was making arrangements for one or two girls, who seemed to be suffering with bad coughs and colds, to be seen by the doctor. Mary was one of them. I was feeling fine by then, having overcome my throat problem and recuperation. However in a conversation a few days earlier I had mentioned that I had slight tingling pains in my legs and had put them down to growing pains, which I had heard about at school.

"Does anyone else need to see the doctor?" Miss Norton shouted. Nobody answered.

"What about you, Mavis Bailey." she continued. "You said that your legs were aching, didn't you?"

"Well, they're not really painful." I replied. "Just a bit of tingling now and again. They are not hurting just now."

She added my name to the list, saying that I would also be seen by the doctor. Privately I thought that this was just to make up the numbers because she wanted Mary to be examined but I knew that I would have to do as I was told.

The doctor, who was actually the senior medical officer in charge, at Stockport health authority, duly arrived, and the girls were presented to him for examination, one by one. I was last.

"Now young lady, what's the matter with you?" he enquired as I stood in front of him.

"Nothing." I answered, but as I heard Miss Norton clear her throat, I quickly added that my legs sometimes tingled a bit.

It was the same doctor who had sent me to hospital a few weeks earlier and he therefore enquired from Miss Norton if I was now fully recovered from the throat infection.

"Yes. She's back at school now." she replied.

Out came his stethoscope as he told me to prepare for examination, which seemingly took forever, as he had me turning this way and that while he listened intently.

"Right. Off you go young lady." he said as I dressed again.

What a waste of time I thought, as I departed. He didn't even ask me about my legs!

Before he left, I was ushered in to see him again and by now Miss Somers was also present.

"Well, Mavis" he began. "It seems your heart is a bit tired!" He had a Scottish accent and I thought I had misheard him. What did he mean, tired? I stared at him.

"It needs to take things easy for a while." he continued. "And the only way we can do that is to see that <u>you</u> take things easy. I'm afraid there'll be no more ping-pong for a wee while!"

My eyes darted to Miss Somers, who had obviously told him of my fondness for table tennis. She was looking at me with a sad expression. I had only just resumed this much- loved activity after my recent bout of sickness and couldn't believe that I was being deprived of it again.

The doctor continued: "The staff here are going to look after you, and you must rest in bed for a bit."

"What does a bit mean?" I asked, not even then thinking that he meant complete rest.

"Well, I'll come to see you again in two weeks time." he responded. "After that, we'll see. But it's important that for two weeks you stay in bed."

Stay in bed? My thoughts raced.

"But I've got to go to school!" I declared. "I've already missed <u>some</u> lessons."

He interrupted. "There will be no school for you for a while my dear. You're going to be a lady of leisure for a bit!"

He indicated that I could now be dismissed and Miss Norton told me to wait in the kitchen. I sat on the church pew, wishing I'd never heard of growing pains!

I was not given any further jobs to do that day and after tea, on the instruction of Miss Somers, I took some magazines to bed. I was still using the attic as my bedroom, not yet having moved back to a dormitory. Mrs. Roberts was away for the weekend.

The implications of the doctor's diagnosis did not hit me until the following morning, Sunday. Miss Norton told me to stay in bed and breakfast was sent up to me. However I had earlier had to get up and go downstairs to use the toilet, situated on the floor below. To have a wash I would have to go down two more flights of stairs to the ablution room, which meant that I would have to climb back up all three, to go back to bed. Miss Norton told me to have a quick wash in the staff bathroom, on the same floor as the toilet, leaving me with only one flight of stairs to climb on my return journey. This was when I began to realise that things were serious. I felt perfectly alright and quite able to go up and down stairs as normal. I felt uncomfortable using the staff bathroom.

Nearly everyone went to church that morning, leaving Miss Somers and two girls to make lunch. Hazel also remained behind but that was normal. She wouldn't behave in church. During the morning Miss Somers brought me tea and biscuits and it was an opportunity for me to bemoan the fact that I was already bored and to plague her with questions. What was wrong with me? Why wasn't I even allowed to go downstairs? What instructions had the doctor given? She answered that all she knew was that I had to get as much rest as possible before the doctor came again and it would be better for all concerned if I co-operated. Mrs. Roberts would be back Monday night and would want to know all the details! After she departed to carry on with her duties I lay there staring at the table tennis kit. The privacy of the attic bedroom had suddenly lost its charm.

* * *

Once Mrs. Roberts returned she lost no time in moving me out of the attic room.

She got the gardener to come indoors the next day and give the staff a hand with moving my bed into her own bedroom, to share it with her. She explained that I couldn't be allowed to go up and down stairs as I was supposed to have complete bed rest. The doctor had suggested that I could be transferred to a sanatorium type hospital if it wasn't convenient to nurse me at The Pines, so surely moving in with her was a better alternative? The toilet was immediately outside her room and I could use the staff bathroom just along the landing, with only two steps to negotiate. I had to agree.

The bedroom was cramped with two beds, but still cosy. Mrs. Roberts' personal belongings were dotted everywhere, and there were mirrors, something I wasn't used to. I stared at myself in them. I didn't look any different!

Everyone was very kind, adults popping in and out to bring me a magazine or a meal, sometimes girls sent to talk to me for a little while, but I was forbidden to get out of bed for any reason other than when nature called. Time dragged on. I wasn't even allowed to knit! Not that I particularly liked knitting, but at least it would have been something to occupy me. I wondered what my friends at school were up to. Were they wondering where I was? I didn't even have any of their addresses to write to them. I wrote to Jack to inform him of my predicament but Mrs. Roberts advised me not to write to my mother just yet. I might be able to get up again next week, no need to upset her, telling her I was confined to bed. I hadn't told my mother that I had been in hospital either.

When the doctor next came to see me, two weeks later, he was delighted with the arrangements made to look after me and congratulated the staff on their initiative. We all knew it was Mrs. Roberts who was the instigator; it was she of course who also lost her privacy with the arrangement. She had realised that the tired heart the doctor talked about was just a way of describing rheumatic fever to me, quite often being preceded by a sceptic throat, as mine had been. I was blissfully unaware that complete rest for several weeks, even months, was the only remedy, as he gently told me to stay where I was for another two weeks, when he would visit me again.

Chapter 26

THE LONG WAIT

I found life very boring for the next few weeks, I had absolutely nothing to do except read. Mrs. Roberts brought me books from the library and supplied me with magazines, bought for herself, and eventually drawing paper was found for me, and I spent my time copying the faces of the models displayed on the front of Woman and Woman's Own magazines. The girls sent to talk to me occasionally, did not really have anything new to tell me, and Hazel, who of course did not go to school, would sometimes during the week, be sent up to deliver a glass of milk to me. She objected to the attention I was receiving and would come barging into the room, march up to the bedside table and set the drink down with a bang, turning on her heels and leaving without speaking! If she was in a black mood, and especially if I attempted to talk to her, she would frustratedly shout at me "BAILEY-BAILEY-BAILEY!!!" as she was leaving.

When the doctor came on his second visit I asked when I could get up out of bed. He replied noncommittally, "Just another week or so."

I knew he was not giving me a straight answer and therefore stressed that I needed to get back to school. I was never going to be able to keep up with the other girls if I didn't! He just smiled, saying "We'll see."

He was far too professional for me to push my luck further, especially with at least one member of staff present. All the staff were in awe of him, feigning heart-flutters when he was around. Miss Norton even asked me if I could draw <u>his</u> face for her. I replied that I could make an attempt if I had a photograph. She supplied one.

Being in such close proximity with Mrs. Roberts had its drawbacks. The bedroom rightly belonged to her but I was in there twenty fours a day, more than she was! She was still encouraging me to look upon her as a second mother and when she wanted to talk about this arrangement I had no escape. When we had been in Bolton she took every opportunity to refer to me as her daughter, for example if we were shopping or meeting people who did not know my background, and even as far back as August when we were at Squires Gate holiday camp, she had made a point of informing new acquaintances, such as the friendly waitress and other guests, that I was special to her.

In the privacy of her bedroom we had several discussions, shedding tears from time to time, about my not referring to her as mother. She pointed out that I had promised to try to use that title but had not done so. She could not understand that I felt that I was betraying my mother. After all, she reasoned, she herself had been placed in exactly the same position when she was young, after her own mother had died and her father had remarried. I was usually so upset that I hadn't the heart to remind her that that was the problem; <u>my</u> mother was still alive.

I couldn't deny however that she was kindness itself to me and I recognised that she deserved to be a mother. She never referred to her late husband dying at such a young age before they had time to become parents. If she referred to him at all it was with a generosity of spirit and fond memories of the short time they had spent together.

* * *

After I had been confined to bed for about six weeks, I received a visit from my friends from school. Miss Robinson had organised it, after school had been informed of the reason for my absence. All three of them were allowed to come once it had been established that I was part of a foursome. They brought grapes, flowers and books and had instructions not to tire me out.

"Tire me out!" I exclaimed. "How can I get tired out? I'm not allowed out of bed!"

"Miss Robinson says that you're delicate and we haven't to overstay on our visit." was the reply. "What's wrong with you again?"

"I don't know." I said exasperatedly. "The doctor hasn't been to see me for ages, but he said at first that I had a tired heart."

"That's not what she said", they all agreed. "She told us you had a fever and there was a possibility that you would <u>never</u> come back to school!"

I laughed. "Well she's got that one wrong," I said. "Do I look as though I've got a fever? I'm as cool as a cucumber."

They were inclined to agree with each other. They were quite certain that she had been deadly serious when giving them their instructions.

They gave me all the gossip from school, even offering the information that one of the boys we used to meet up with in Woolworth's at lunchtimes and who made no secret of the fact that I was his favourite, had now turned his attention to someone else. I brushed this news aside with a shrug, privately thinking that the relationship between us had never stood a chance of developing beyond lunchtimes anyhow. He had asked to see me several times at weekends and I had always made an excuse.

Our form was almost ready to take Easter exams now and my friends chatted about new shorthand and typing speeds they had attained and various other preparations they were making for exams. I asked why they hadn't brought <u>me</u> some of their latest work to look at, as we normally discussed all lessons together. They replied once again that they had been forbidden to do so. Consequently conversation between us was limited.

They told me that they had to report back to school before going home, as they had been given the afternoon off to enable them to visit me. Miss Robinson wanted them back in school before closure for the day and they had been given bus fare and a bus timetable, and so they kept a wary eye on the clock. The time passed all too quickly for me.

After they had departed, saying that they would do their best to come again, I was in a forlorn mood when Mrs. Roberts returned to the bedroom, having seen them off the premises. She bustled about, checking if there was anything I needed.

"Miss Robinson sent them." I said, by way of explanation. "They said that Miss Robinson has told them that I won't be going back to school, but I will won't I? Once the doctor has been again and finds out that I've had all this rest. He'll let me go then won't he?"

She had avoided my gaze so far, but now she hesitated and then came to sit by my side.

"Actually, you've got a lot more rest in store yet." she said gently.

"What kind of rest?" I demanded. "I'll be able to get out of bed won't I?"

"Not until the doctor says it's alright for you to do so," she countered. "It could take quite a few more weeks yet."

I was appalled, and suddenly I knew that I had been deliberately misled.

"You've all known from the beginning haven't you?" I shouted. "No wonder he hasn't been to see me for a while. When is he coming again?"

"Well, the last time he saw you he said he would come again in a month." she answered.

I did a rapid calculation; that means he won't be here for another fortnight, I thought.

I groaned. Mrs. Roberts interrupted my thoughts.

"If I had known they were going to tell you, I wouldn't have let them come," she said.

I shrugged her away as my tears welled up and she attempted to comfort me.

* * *

I had to come to terms with this newly found information and in an effort to make life as interesting as possible for me, Mrs. Roberts did her best to make arrangements for other people to visit me. Always writing letters I was able to keep in touch with my three brothers, as well as writing to my mother, and my brothers all came to visit me at different times. Miss Somers too brought her niece Jean to visit me and we were able to do jig-saw puzzles together and play board games. She also arranged for the Major at the Salvation Army citadel to visit me. He and his wife had got to know me quite well when I went to the young people's recreation group and also at Sunday evening services with Miss Somers. Everyone was very kind but time dragged on as I gazed out of the window and watched the trees come into bud.

The doctor's visits were now more or less on a monthly basis and the frustrating thing to me was the fact that no-one would allow me to do anything without his permission. Consequently no progress was made between visits.

My mother answered my letters, continually asking me to make sure that Bill went to see her. She was still having alternate monthly visits between Jack and Bill, with aunt Edith fitting in with one or the other. She was also aware that I had not been to see her for a long time and mentioned this in her letters to me. Of course it was not only the current year so far that I had not been able to visit her, I had also missed out in the latter part of the previous year. I still had not told her that I was confined to bed, but I endeavoured to make sure that from my letters she knew that I was thinking about her. I made both my brothers promise that they would give her my love, and confirm that both Clifford and I were alright.

* * *

I was still struggling with the problem of knowing how much Mrs. Roberts cared for me, showing me love and support in many ways, yet I still couldn't bring myself to address her in the way she desired. I couldn't even <u>think</u> of her as being my mother; I still had a mother. I didn't feel that I could talk to Miss Somers about it either, as they were such close friends. In desperation I decided to write to an agony aunt to ask for advice. I chose Mary Grant, agony aunt for Woman's Own magazine.

I secretly wrote my letter, explaining my situation as best I could, and stressing what a wonderful caring woman Mrs. Roberts was. I explained that I was at a complete loss to know how to return the love and consideration she showed to me, without feeling that I was betraying my own mother. I decided to be very frank and confess that what I really wanted was my own mother back again, but that Mrs. Roberts would always have a special place in my life, because I knew that she loved me. In conclusion I asked Mary Grant not to publish my letter, as Mrs. Roberts would read it and feel very hurt; I did not wish to hurt her. I asked for a reply by post.

Once I had written the letter I waited for a suitable opportunity for Margaret, the The Pines girl with the copper- coloured hair, to come to pass some time with me and then asked her if she would post a letter for me on her way to Sunday school. Falsely indicating that I had not yet written the letter, I asked her if she would come to collect it on Sunday, by which time I would have written it. I concocted a story of how I didn't want the adults to know that I had written to the magazine and asked her not to tell anyone. She agreed and everything went as planned. It was to be nearly a month before I received a reply, and by then I had ceased to wait for the anticipated delivery. I had presumed that just as certain letters were selected for printing in the magazine, the same procedure probably applied to postal replies.

The month had dragged on with little change. Two of my friends paid me one more visit but we didn't really have much to talk about, especially from my point of view, and they couldn't stay long enough to attempt to play board games.

The doctor didn't turn up when he was due, and even the staff began eventually to agree with me that he was keeping a low profile! Each day became monotonous.

When Mrs. Roberts went home for weekends I was glad to have her bedroom to myself, but equally I was just as pleased when she came back again. She always brought me news and letters from home.

April arrived and a further letter from my mother. The letters she sent were never really cheerful and I guessed that many times Mrs. Roberts would give them to me with some trepidation. I didn't usually show her the letters unless I was proving some point or other, but I read them over and over again trying to glean any new information I could from them. She would often come into the room and find me pouring over a letter, and she would ask in a deliberately casual manner how my mother was. I knew she meant well and she herself must have felt that she was 'treading on egg shells' but the relationship between us over this one aspect was deteriorating. I was unwilling to let her in to my troubled thoughts. After all she had never met my mother, whom I loved above anyone else, and I knew that she would never be able to take her place.

The following is a typical example of my mother's letters at the time.

Ward 14, Main,
Whittingham
Nr. Preston.
April 13th, 1950

Dear Mavis,

Just a line in answer to your ever loving letter, sorry I haven't answered it before.

Well Mavis, I do hope you come on Saturday, also our Bill and Jack. It's a good while since you came. I am longing to see you.

I hope you bring me something nice. I don't get any money at all now and I miss my five shillings very much.

Please tell our Bill I do want to see him. I am sure it's over a month since he came. Don't forget to tell him will you?

I think this is all for now and hope to hear from or see you very soon.

I am your ever loving Mother, XXXXXXXXX
Goodnight and God Bless you,
Mum. XXXXXXXXXXXX

A previous letter she had sent to me in March was almost identical and I realised that like me she had nothing to write about. She still did not know that I was confined to bed and unable to visit her. When writing to her I refrained from mentioning visits to the hospital, always hoping that the next time I saw the doctor he would let me get up.

* * *

It was early one afternoon when I received the answering letter from Mary Grant. I had enclosed a stamped addressed envelope with my letter to her and recognised it immediately when Miss Norton took it out of her apron pocket as she entered the bedroom. Her eyes did not meet mine as she gave it to me saying: "A letter for you Mavis." She did not show any further interest in it as she turned around after giving it to me, and left the room. The letter had a clear London postmark.

I knew instantly from her demeanour that she had read it, and my heart started to pound! This was the very last thing

I wanted. I had not anticipated it at all. How could I have been so stupid! Even the time of delivery confirmed what I had already worked out. She had had the letter long enough to steam open the envelope to read it, even if it had arrived that same day, but it could have come anytime. I normally received my letters mid-morning, but she had deliberately chosen a quiet time to give it to me, just after lunch. Mrs. Roberts would be downstairs with Matron just then.

I was too devastated to read the letter for a little while and of course I didn't want to be unexpectedly discovered reading it.

When I finally got around to reading it I was even more dismayed. It was quite apparent what the subject matter was and who it referred to. I couldn't really concentrate on the advice Mary Grant was attempting to give to me, for trying to find out what information Miss Norton had been able to glean from it and would she at any time use it as ammunition against Mrs. Roberts, who had stood up to her several times on my behalf. I was aware of the underlying friction existing between Miss Norton and the rest of the staff. I groaned inwardly, what to do next?

I felt very guilty when Mrs. Roberts, smiling as ever, brought me afternoon tea and biscuits later on. I knew she would be dreadfully upset if she thought that Miss Norton was sharing our intimate thoughts, even though I had no control over it. I should never have written to Mary Grant! At first glance the letter did not tell me anything I didn't know anyway.

* * *

In a curious way, the fact that Miss Norton could consider that she now had an advantage over Mrs. Roberts, made me very protective. At the first opportunity I had, I brought into conversation with Mrs. Roberts the 'unmentionable' subject of our relationship. I could tell that she was surprised but she readily responded in a pleasant manner. I told her that I had been thinking about things she had said to me and although I wanted to think of her in a motherly way, I still found it very hard to say the word. She surprised me by saying that she understood that very well, and that she knew someone who called her mother 'Mum'. Did I think that I could manage that?

It was the perfect answer. To me, even though my own mother had recently used it as a postscript in a letter to me, that was the only time I had ever known her to use that particular endearment, and she would always remain 'Mother' to me. As young children we had called her 'Mam' a northern term generally used in the 1930's and 1940's, but we had always referred to her as 'Mother', especially in writing.

I knew then that Mrs. Roberts and I had found the solution. I hid the offending letter in my personal possessions, knowing that she would not intrude my private space, nor I hers. When my birthday arrived at the beginning of May, she was able to send me a greetings card signed - 'From Mum, with love.' I didn't mind at all, it was a term of endearment unique to her and I gradually learned to use it more often. Our relationship improved tremendously.

Chapter 27

HAZEL

By May I had been confined to bed for more than three months and was feeling pretty fed up. When the doctor came early that month he at last, after much pleading, said I could get out of bed, under supervision, for approximately one hour each day, and he would come to see me again in two weeks time. I could not leave the bedroom, apart from necessary ablutions. I was disappointed with the time scale but acknowledged that at least it was a start. I was not allowed to get dressed as it was considered to be too active. Indeed by the time I had usually taken a bath (never alone) I would often feel exhausted and be glad to sit in a chair whilst someone dried and curled my hair.

The days began to get longer and sunnier as the month wore on and I began to think that, maybe after his next visit, the doctor might even let me sit in the sunshine in the garden for a bit. No such luck. The two- week period extended into four, so it was early June before I saw him again.

In the meantime Mrs. Roberts had promised the children that she would take them on a picnic during their spring holiday from school at the end of May and they were all looking forward to this, as preparations were made over the preceding period. Miss Norton would not be on duty at that particular time but Miss Somers agreed to help in any way she could, and if necessary they could recruit Miss Finch who still acted as a 'staff floater' between the three children's homes. The picnic involved taking all twenty or so children by bus to the designated beauty spot, so it would need at least two staff to control them. Then there was the problem of me. We had all been hoping to ask the doctor if I could go along as well, providing I took things easy, but he had not visited as promised.

The final plan was for Miss Finch to accompany Mrs. Roberts, and Miss Somers would stay with me. It didn't happen; Miss Finch was needed elsewhere and rather than disappoint the children I suggested that I would be perfectly alright by myself, after all I was now fifteen years old. This needed thinking about! Maybe if one of the older girls stayed behind with me it might work.

Not one of the girls wanted to miss the picnic and I didn't blame them. Treats like this were few and far between. It was the freedom to do something different that was the attraction; life otherwise was routinely boring.

The day when it arrived was gloriously sunny, perfect for the occasion, and Mrs. Roberts and Miss Somers could not disappoint the children. However they were also having problems with Hazel, who, being in a dark mood, and not really knowing what a picnic was about, decided she wasn't going to be made to go, and dug her heels in!

We had all experienced this stubborn attitude before and knew that she would have to be ignored until she had come through the mood.

Eventually the two staff persuaded her that she could be really helpful if she stayed at The Pines with me. Would she like to remain behind in charge of things? Of course the thought of being in charge suited Hazel very well as she was still very jealous of the attention I received, but actually the staff were more concerned about leaving her than they were about leaving me. I stressed that I would be perfectly alright and knew how to handle Hazel. Reluctantly they left the two of us with a picnic of our own, to be taken in the bedroom, and with a nod and a wink to me, gave Hazel her 'instructions' on how to look after me. Neither of us had to go downstairs, most rooms were being locked before their departure anyhow.

All went well for a time as I tried to think of things to keep Hazel occupied. Board games and reading were out of the question, also knitting or embroidery but she still carried her kaleidoscope around with her and being of sturdy construction this had remained remarkably intact; I was surprised when she agreed to my taking a look. The patterns were certainly beautiful. She also loved to play 'I spy' but of course never knew the first letter of any object so her opponent had to make wild guesses. Hazel usually got bored first and would stomp across the room, shouting out the name of the object. Hunt the thimble was also played in this manner but the hidden object was never really hidden, she just liked the thrill of getting warmer and warmer!

After we had eaten our picnic I suggested that I should now have a rest in bed, and if <u>she</u> would like to lie down on the remaining bed, I was sure that Mrs. Roberts wouldn't mind. I made the mistake of saying that when we had had a little rest we would be able to do some crayoning. Hazel wasn't tired anyway. She had huge reserves of energy and lying on a bed in the middle of the day was not for her! Hardly any time passed at all before she wanted to crayon pictures; when five or ten minutes on the bed were up I had no option other than to accommodate her.

She quickly got bored with the crayons and in desperation I told her to go up into the attic and look for something to play with. She came down again with a table tennis bat and ball. Of course it was my undoing; I sent her up again to get a bat for me!

She was gone for what seemed an age and I could not hear her moving about, or returning. Eventually I walked down the landing to the bottom of the flight of stairs leading to the attic, and shouted her name. No answer. I knew then that she was up to something but couldn't get her to come out of the room. I waited, trying to figure out what could be fascinating her. I didn't think it would be the sewing machine as this was always kept locked. It must be the doll's house, normally off limits to the children. If it <u>was</u> the doll's house, I realised that the furniture wouldn't last long if she were to lose her temper. I decided to leave her for a bit longer, hoping she would come down of her own accord.

After ten minutes or so I made my way to the foot of the stairs and shouted again. She appeared at the top, laughing. I knew this was because she had done something she knew was wrong.

"What have you been doing Hazel?" I asked. "Have you been playing with the doll's house?" She nodded.

"Come on down now Hazel." I said. "And bring another bat, I'll play with you."

Of course I meant just a gentle knock-about in the bedroom, but still laughing she refused to come.

"I w-w-want you to come here!" she declared, and when I told her that I couldn't, in frustration she shouted the usual "BAILEY-BAILEY-BAILEY!!!" stomping toward the attic and closing the door with a bang!

I had two options. I could either leave her up there until everyone came back or I could go up to her. If I left her the black mood was liable to get worse, and that could happen whilst I was still on my own, or I could go upstairs and confront her, as I had done many times in the past, turning her attention away from herself. I decided to do the latter.

I did not find the stairs a problem, even though this particular flight was rather steep. I took my time, not making any noise, eventually arriving at the attic door and pushing it open. Hazel was standing in the middle of the room in a defiant attitude, the like of which I had seen many times previously. The doll's house front was swinging open and one hinge seemed to be broken. Immediately in front of me was the erected table for table tennis, and bats were lying on top of it. She pointed to the doll's house, saying that she hadn't done it!

"No, it was already broken." I said casually. She stopped flailing her arms. I turned away as if it was of no consequence and she followed me. We reached the table and I picked up a bat.

"This is what you came up here for Hazel." I said, taking pleasure in the feel of the handle. "Is there a ball?" She immediately found one and gave it to me.

"Pick up that other bat then." I continued "And I'll knock the ball to you."

Surprisingly she knew the stance to adopt but couldn't quite return the ball I sent to her. I tried again, and again, making her retrieve the ball each time.

I'll be alright if I just stand here knocking the ball, my thoughts deluded me. I'll just make sure Hazel is out of her mood before we go back downstairs.

Even playing with Hazel, who did in the end manage to return the ball a few times, was better than not playing at all and I gave no thought to the consequences.

After a while I knew that Hazel's mood had passed and as I was feeling a bit weak by then, I suggested that we went down to my bedroom for chocolate!

"It's not your b-b-bedroom!" she stated sharply. "It's Mrs. R-R-Roberts' bedroom. Nevertheless she agreed that she would like some chocolate.

"We can play cards as well." I said, knowing that she couldn't play card games but particularly liked to look at the picture face-cards with their two heads. Making allowances for her I could sometimes get her to play Snap with them, always letting her win of course. Usually on my own I played games of Patience.

I was more than ready to lie down when we returned to the bedroom and she was happy enough eating the chocolate and staring at her reflection in the mirror. After a while, after first sending her back to the attic with the 'tell-tale' bat and ball from the bedroom, I propped myself up with pillows and we played with the cards.

Not long afterwards everyone returned, Hazel was the first to hear them arrive, and jumped up shouting with glee. Both Mrs. Roberts and Miss Somers came up to see me almost immediately and I could tell they were relieved to discover a calm atmosphere. They had not stayed out as long as they would have liked, they knew they shouldn't have left us alone and had tried to do their best by everyone. I assured them that everything had been fine whilst they were out. Having previously instructed Hazel not to tell anyone that she had been in the attic playroom, I didn't mention it either, hoping for the best.

It was the next morning before the misdeed came to light. Someone discovered the broken front of the doll's house and questions were raised. Hazel vehemently denied that she had done it.

"It wasn't me, it was Mavis Bailey," she claimed.

One thing led to another of course and she insisted that she had seen me break it.

I was not present when this conversation was taking place but eventually Mrs. Roberts came to me to check out for herself whether or not I had really been upstairs, and I had to confess. That was bad enough for her to be extremely disappointed in me but when, thinking that Hazel had mentioned this too, I admitted to playing table-tennis, she sank down on the bed with a look of horror.

We discussed the events rationally but she was very concerned. She understood how I had at first gone to cope with Hazel's mood, and that was bad enough, but to throw caution to the wind and be so active for such a period was really going to set me back.

"You must have known you were asking for trouble," she stated. "How did you feel at the time? Were you short of breath?"

I had been perfectly alright once I had gone back to bed and rested, although I <u>had</u> been glad to lie down, and so I told her that I had had no ill effects at all.

"We will have to tell the doctor," she said resignedly. "I don't know what he'll say!"

Privately I thought that we shouldn't have to tell him, we could just wait to see what he said after the next examination, whenever that happened, but refrained from saying so. The matter was eventually dropped. I think both members of staff felt guilty at having left me alone with Hazel, but I had encouraged them to do so.

In time we would laugh about the incident, how Hazel had turned the tables on me!

Chapter 28

BOLTON.

When children in care in the 1950's reached school leaving age, employment had to be found for them by the local council, and this had to include 'live-in' facilities. Consequently most children finished up in domestic service, where accommodation was provided with the job; the young person was then monitored by the child-care officers from the authority, until the age of eighteen. My predecessor at The Pines, the teenager who had left before I arrived, had been an exception to this rule. The Pines itself had had a vacancy for domestic assistance at the time, and so she remained there, employed thus. This was the girl, I discovered later, that both Mrs. Roberts and Miss Somers felt had been unfairly treated. She had been paid a meagre wage, had used the attic as a bedroom, and had simply carried on with the drudgery of household duties but on a full-time basis. She had been allowed out in her free time but under a strict timetable rule. This was one of the reasons that Mrs. Roberts had usually objected whenever I had to use the attic as a bedroom, and why, until the incident at the cinema, she had been instrumental in making sure I went on independent excursions when I became old enough. Unknown to me at the time, she was also determined that I should not become a domestic servant.

I had never given much thought as to where I would live when I left The Pines. I think this was in part due to the fact that my school-life, where employment would have been eventually discussed towards school-leaving age, had come to an abrupt halt. I always presumed that I would get better and resume school once again, and I suppose I thought that this would be the time to think about my future. In addition of course I lived in eternal hope that my mother would also get better and we could resume our lives together.

Mrs. Roberts however had been thinking about my future for some time, and had in fact made provisional arrangements with her own mother that when the time was right she would offer me a home with her, at Bolton. The idea was that I would find employment, live with her mother under her supervision, backed up by Bolton child-care authority. Mrs. Roberts would remain in Stockport to finish her career, spending her free time at Bolton as usual. She had begun to seek permission with the authorities involved long before she put the idea to me.

When I became ill however, this was a further obstacle to the plan, which was therefore put on hold until the Stockport medical officer for health, (my own doctor, as it happened) gave his permission to proceed.

On his next visit I was apprehensive about his reaction to my excursion up to the attic with Hazel, but after a lengthy examination it was determined that no great harm had been done and that after a further week's rest I could be allowed up for part of the day. School was not on the agenda. He would come to visit me again in two or three weeks time. This would take us to the end of June, and it was then that I realised that I would not be going back to school again, as I would be due to finish altogether in late July.

Having obtained permission from all sources, Mrs. Roberts now put the idea to me, pointing out that before any decision could be made we ought to discuss it from every aspect, as in the end, the final decision would be whether or not I would want to leave Stockport, and in any case I had to be fully recovered in health before it would be allowed.

It didn't take me long to reach my decision. I knew that there was a home for me at Bolton and that I would be made to feel welcome. I could hardly believe that life was going to get good again for me.

Next, we had to at least inform my relatives of my desire to leave Stockport, even if we didn't ask their permission. They might even have ideas of their own to offer me a home. Earlier in the year Clifford had been sent to live with foster carers, where it was felt he would benefit from a normal home background whilst still attending the grammar school. The people fostering him were paid for their role and the term used to describe such an arrangement was 'to be boarded out'. There would be no such boarding out fee paid on my behalf once I had obtained a job.

It took me a week or so to come to terms with the idea of living at Bolton, but from my previous visits I knew that it wasn't exactly the other side of the world and once I had settled and got a job earning my own money I could travel back to see Clifford as much as possible. I knew also that it was perfectly possible to visit my mother by bus from Bolton and that I would be able to do this on a regular basis, under my own steam. I would also be able to keep in touch with my other brothers. The whole idea seemed absolutely perfect to me.

June and July were spent increasing my activity day by day, Mrs. Roberts ensuring that I did not exert myself unduly. We had private celebrations when at last I was allowed downstairs and eventually outside into the garden. On one occasion, in the dining room, I was standing idly by while Miss Norton, accompanied by Mary, was lightly sweeping the floor after we children had eaten. She asked me if I would like to take a turn and I eagerly accepted, it was not in my nature to be idle. Someone must have sped off to inform Mrs. Roberts who was in the kitchen, because in next to no time she was present in the dining room, relieving me of the brush and rebuking Miss Norton for her thoughtless attitude in recruiting me for work. I almost felt sorry for Miss Norton as she tried in vain to convince Mrs. Roberts that she was only letting me do what I seemed to want.

At last I was allowed to travel and I was able to visit Bolton once again. Mum, as I now called Mrs. Roberts was in her element taking me to visit various relatives and informing them of the impending arrangements. Her mother's doctor however was not in agreement with the idea and after being approached by the local authority for medical approval of his patient to be fit to look after me, lost no time in visiting her to admonish her for her ill thought out plan. She made arrangements for him to meet me and he was won over! No doubt Mrs. Roberts had a hand in that too.

By August it was deemed that I was fit enough to move to Bolton and be placed under the care of Bolton authority, who would arrange monitoring from time to time. I also had to find a doctor and a job.

Mum came with me and saw that I was settled in with her mother before she had to return to The Pines. Once again the children were going to the holiday camp at Squires Gate for their annual holiday and Mrs. Roberts and Miss Somers were the staff chosen to go on this occasion. Having left The Pines I was no longer eligible for this excursion. It didn't bother me in the slightest. Clifford would not be going either.

Leaving The Pines had not been difficult. There were no tearful good-byes, just genuine good wishes from Miss Somers, whom I knew I would be seeing again anyhow; she was now my friend as well as Mum's.

* * *

Mrs. Roberts' mother quickly became known as 'Grandma' to me. We got along well together. She had strict old-fashioned ideas, which in the fullness of time were mellowed, and she was very religious. No knitting or embroidery on Sunday! This must have been very difficult for her as she spent the main part of every other day doing just that. Sundays were spent at her own church, a different one from the nearby church that Mum and her sister attended, and which they took me to as well.

When Mum wasn't there I went with her sister, Jenny.

Grandma approved of my independent attitude and knew that I wasn't lazy. We had great respect for each other, getting over the various small problems we both encountered living together. Jenny helped a great deal and often had to remind me that it was after all her mother's home, and things were changing all the time, not always to her mother's liking. I learned to be more tolerant.

For the first time in several years I had a real home again, surrounded by caring people. Jenny, who was at that time in her late twenties, permanently waved my straight hair with a Toni perm, very popular at the time, and taught me how to use light make-up, making my whole appearance look well-cared for but not brash. She supplied the make-up etc. and gave me advice on how to dress as a young adult.

My first job, obtained through a youth employment scheme, was a very junior clerk in the dairy department of the local Co-operative Society; my work entailed logging deliveries of dairy products to the many branch stores in and around Bolton. My newly found 'foster relatives' were very pleased on my behalf with such employment. Their attitude was - a job with the Co-op. was a job for life, but although I put my best effort into it, I found it very humdrum in a dilapidated building. I think the idea was that one started at the bottom and the Society, being so very large, could then offer you more suitable employment through the future years. Hardly any shorthand and typing were involved and I knew that to keep up my speeds I had to have daily practice in addition to my night-school classes for commerce, in which I had enrolled at the beginning of the autumn term.

During this time Mum came home several times and we were always pleased to see each other. In addition I could telephone her from a nearby telephone kiosk. In the past when I had been at The Pines, she used to bring me news from Bolton, now it was the opposite, she brought news from The Pines. On her first visit after staying at Squires Gate holiday camp with the children, she brought intriguing news.

Apparently during their stay at the camp they had been served in the dining room by Lorna, the waitress who had become so friendly with Mum the previous year. Mum was delighted to see her and was somewhat surprised to be met with a rather cool reception. Next, Mum noticed that Lorna was wearing a wedding ring and showed delight and surprise, congratulating her and naturally asking when the wedding had taken place. It turned out to have been New Year's Eve.

"I sent you a letter." Lorna said. "Telling you when it would be and asking if Mavis could be my bridesmaid."

Of course Mum was stunned at this news and wanted Lorna to understand that she had never received it.

"I didn't get it Lorna," she said. "Whom did you address it to and what address did you use?"

She had addressed it to The Person in Charge, at The Pines. When she didn't get a reply she wrote again, stressing that the date of the wedding was fast approaching, and asking for a decision. She never received a reply, even though she had sent both letters to the correct address.

Another letter that had gone astray! Mum had to explain as best she could that neither she nor I even knew that Lorna had set a date for the wedding.

Mum was furious, as of course the previous New Year's Eve was before my sceptic throat and I would have been well enough to attend the wedding; it would have been a pleasure to be a bridesmaid for Lorna. She filled her in with details about my illness and how at the present time I was just beginning my new life at Bolton.

When she got back to The Pines and tackled Miss Norton about the letter, she denied all knowledge of it.

* * *

I was paid a very modest wage for my first job and so my income was supplemented by an amount from the children's care department of the local authority, in order to make sure I had a living wage to pay for overheads and food. I was lucky in that I was able to give Grandma my weekly wage and then she fed me and put money aside for clothing etc. She also had to take into account more overheads in order to meet my needs, but I always got the residue for my spending money. I had to find travelling expenses to and from work from this as well as treats for myself but my main aim at the beginning was to save a percentage for bus fare to visit my mother.

I still continued to write to her and also kept in touch with Jack by 'phoning him at work and so I knew the visiting roster. Jack came on his motorcycle to collect me on my first visit, as I had not been for a long time. It was wonderful to see her but I could tell that she had deteriorated over the intervening months, and looked much older, her spirit finally broken. She was of course equally delighted to see me: she had been expecting aunt Edith instead, who usually went by bus, meeting Jack at the hospital. I was thankful that she didn't ask me why I had not visited for so long, for although she knew that I now lived at Bolton I never told her the extent of my illness.

I went to see her again the following month, boarding a bus at Bolton with Preston as its destination. As I entered the top deck I could see my brother Bill sitting half way along the bus, having boarded at Stockport. He had no idea that I would also be visiting, although I had guessed that he would be, and after the usual greeting between siblings there was not much conversation between us. We had not seen each other for several months and small-talk was difficult. In addition he had upset me at the outset of our journey together, when he asked me why I had not let him know that I would be visiting mother, as it wasn't necessary for both of us to go, he would not have made the journey. At that time I did not have the courage to rebuke him for his thoughtless attitude, I was fifteen years old, he was in his early thirties. However I took advantage of the fact that he was with me that day; he was able to help me renew my knowledge of the journey from Preston to the hospital. I had only been by bus once before, with aunt Edith.

Chapter 29

CONCLUSION.

I began to enjoy my life at Bolton. I had a good home, became more independent every day and kept up a good relationship with Mum even though her work meant that she was at Stockport more than Bolton. Not only did I have the caring people who surrounded me, such as Grandma, Mum and Jenny, I was also made welcome into their extended families, and the family parties which I had experienced the previous Christmas were still held from time to time. I also made new friends of my own age group both from church activities, night school, and learning how to dance at a school for dancing, before venturing into the local dance halls. All this took time of course, covering many months.

After spending three or four months working for the Co-operative Society, I found a different job. I became junior clerk at a family-run timber merchants and stayed for several years, progressing steadily. I really enjoyed my work and was rewarded with a good salary and any help and assistance I needed by all the staff, both in my personal and working life.

Whilst I was employed thus, Mum was furthering her own career back in Stockport.

She became senior housemother at a newly formed children's home for children of all ages and regardless of sex. This meant that in many cases siblings were able to stay together. Mum was now equal to Miss Norton in rank and recruited Miss Somers as an assistant, in addition to new staff.

I visited this home many times and always found a loving, easy-going atmosphere, where the children seemed to be as happy as possible, considering the upheaval that had obviously taken place when they were taken into care. Mum was rewarded with job satisfaction.

I continued to visit my own mother on a regular basis, regardless of who else would be there, but as I grew older I began to realise that there wasn't much chance of our making a home together, in the immediate future at least. Bill had a wife and young family to support and didn't seem inclined to offer her a home, which would also entail nursing care. Jack was still lodging with aunt Edith, but in any case would be recruited into the armed forces for national service at the age of twenty one for two years, I was also, in effect, lodging with kind but unrelated people, and Clifford, still a schoolboy was still in the care of Stockport authority. I knew the future looked bleak for my mother.

When she died in 1951 from a cerebral haemorrhage, at the age of only 52, she had already suffered the indignities of the mental hospital for almost four years. After my visits to her I would despairingly cry myself to sleep, asking God why he was letting her suffer for so long. How could I object then, when He seemingly answered my prayers, by taking her?

She was laid to rest in the same grave as my father on a wet October day, under a headstone of Re-united, and I was inconsolable at the graveside. Through my tears I observed, unexpectedly, Mum and Miss Somers standing a little way off, sharing an umbrella. I was surprised that they had found details of the funeral in order to attend and realised that they had come out of respect for a woman they didn't know. It must have been very hard for Mum to see me so upset and to stay in the background. She did not approach any of us. Clifford did not have any such support, apart from immediate family.

* * *

I continued to thrive in my new environment and as the years passed I was to meet my husband and have my own children, who would look upon my foster mother as their rightful grandmother. She, of course, inherited what she always wanted, a daughter of her own and grandchildren whom she adored, and who loved her in return. Mum herself was eventually to re-marry and so, along with my husband's parents, my children had two sets of grandparents when growing up.

I am a grandmother myself now, still happily married to my children's father, and although we have lost many loved ones over the years, and our own demise gets ever closer, we both agree that we have been lucky with our parentage both in the blood-lines and in my case, foster care. If it hadn't been made possible by Mum, my foster mother, I would never have come to Bolton and met my husband, resulting in my beautiful children and grandchildren.

My only regret is that my own dear mother never met them.